living on the earth

celebrations,
storm warnings, formulas,
recipes, rumors, & country dances
harvested by alicia bay laurel

vintage books · a division of random house · new york

if you leave this paper in the sun it turns a creamy yellow.

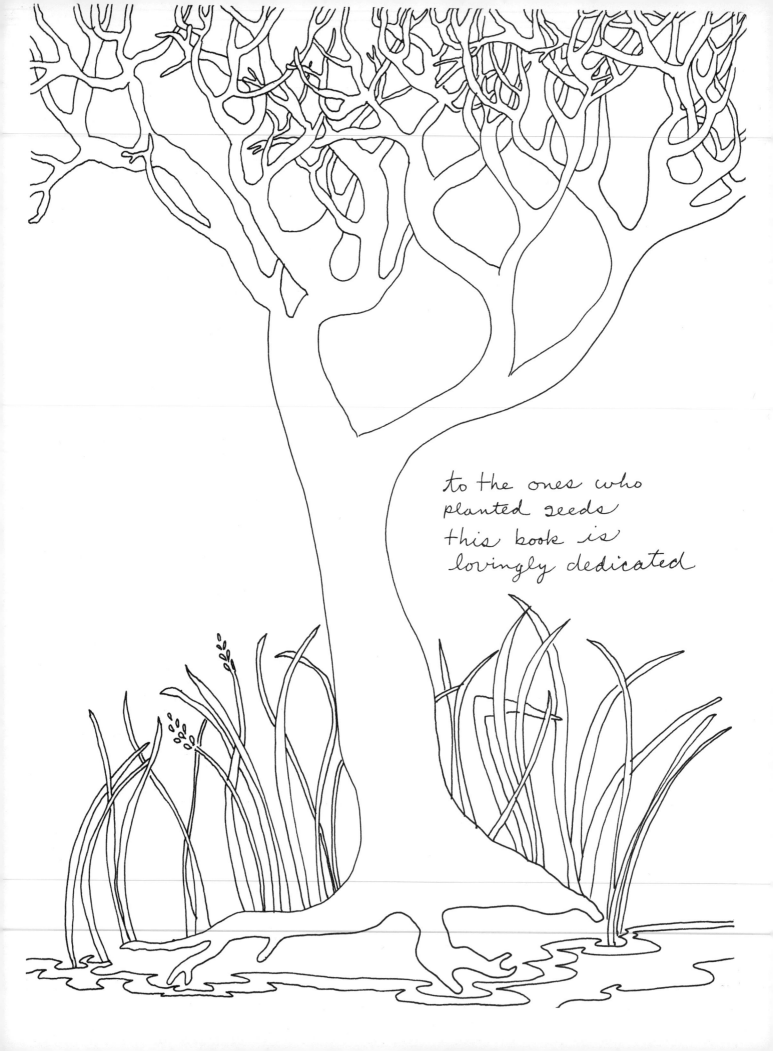

to the ones who
planted seeds
this book is
lovingly dedicated

I would like to
thank my friends at Wheeler's
Ranch for making this book
grow. I would like to especially
mention some people whose energy
inspired these pages:

ramon & joan
bill & gay & raspberry
brice & charlotte
josh & ellie
john & sue
errol & sarah
moses, adam, anne,
peggy, charlie, heidi
pam & faith
phil & lennie
alan lesstoil
christina & terry

bill & sheila
peter & nancy
tony & jane
joseph & anna
saul & harmony
lou & rina
bee & bea
daric & sam
chloe
sid
gerine
esther

I love you all.

introduction
. . . .

this book is for people who
would rather chop wood than
work behind a desk so they can pay
P. G. & E. It has no chapters; it just
grew as I learned; you may find the
index your only guide to this unmapped
land. However, if you have a feeling
for the flow of things, you will discover
a path: from traveling the wilds to the
first fence, simple housing, furnishing
houses, crafts, agriculture, food
preparation, medicine — not unlike the
development of our ancient ancestors.

When we depend less on industrially
produced consumer goods, we can

live in quiet places.
Our bodies become
vigorous ; we discover
the serenity of living
with the rhythms of
the earth. We cease
oppressing one another.

I hope you will write to
me so that I can learn more.
"bay laurel" is not my
parents' surname but
it is my favorite tree.

Alicia bay laurel

weather is   fair — cumulus clouds passing through

dark nimbus clouds piling up into thunderheads

dense stratus clouds hang over the whole sky

high transparent cirrus clouds are made of ice crystals

the cumulus clouds can form waves or rows of
small clouds called "mackerel sky" — changing weather.

backpacking is beauty & discovery or a painful ordeal depending on how you are prepared for it. You must be in good condition physically. Take short hikes to put your body in that rhythm. When you go to a high altitude, spend 3 days getting acclimated before you attempt a long hike. Especially be prepared when you go above the timber line. Tell the forest rangers before you go, so they know you're up there if you have trouble.

Take: Salt to prevent body dehydration (in high altitudes) a hat & lotion to protect against sunburn & windburn, toilet paper & plastic bags, sheath or scout knife first aid: antiseptic, bandage (tape & gauze), needle candles, matches in a watertight container, plastic canteen, map, compass, plastic fold-up raincoat (not a pancho)

Hiking. Pick your own rhythm. Don't go faster than you want to; it's better to go slowly and make few stops than to hasten and make many stops. Start early in the morning.

Safety. Don't hike alone.
Don't go above the timber line
if the weather is not fair;
thunderstorms up there are
very dangerous. Don't try
to climb on ice or snow
unless you have the
proper equipment. Don't
roll rocks downhill or shout
unless you really need
help. Don't slide down
snowbanks. Watch out
for falling rocks. Turn
back if your strength
fails; if clothing or equipment
is inadequate, if the
climb is too hazardous
or if bad weather or
night comes.

equipment: for a one day hike, a small knapsack with a lunch, an extra sweater and the items listed under "take" should be enough.
for camping, especially above the timberline, you will need more:

Pack frame: choose one that rides well on you, is the correct size, and has good balance, lightness, durability and ability to shed rain. On the frame place your equipment each in its own plastic bag. Cover with a plastic sheet and lash it together with rope. This takes more practice than just packing your things into a sack, but this way you can pack for better balance and it is more organized. Carry less than 25 pounds.

sleeping bag the best kind for backpacking is a double thickness down-filled mummy bag. (2 bags that fit one inside the other - water resistant but not water proof). Sierra Designs of Berkeley has mummy bags for two.

tent: the best tent for high altitude backpacking is made of nylon pima cloth with 6 inch stakes of aluminum. If it doesn't have a floor, get an army-type poncho of nylon impregnated with rubber to use as a ground cloth. The poncho has many uses, but it is too clumsy to use as a raincoat for mountain hiking.

other equipment: 2 nesting pots & fry pan (U.S. Army "mountain kit=) a glove (potholder), spatula, spoons, forks, plates (plastic or aluminum), steel wool, plastic cups, can opener, one-burner camping stove for above timberline, a grate (rack) for below it, rope, a wiskbroom (sounds fussy, but it's very handy for cleaning out the tent quickly), light hand axe for wood & for driving tent stakes, light spade or shovel for leveling tent area and digging fire pit & shit holes. You may want binoculars, a camera, pencil & paper, dark glasses, flashlight.

clothing: blue jeans or wool whipcord trousers, tee shirt, 2 or 3 light weight long sleeve shirts of wool or nylon to don & doff as weather dictates, waterproof or water resistant jacket that goes below the waist, hat or bandana light cotton socks and over them 2 pairs of light wool socks or one heavy pair ½ size too big. Clothes should not fit tightly nor should they be bulky.

boots: in dry country, sneakers are fine, but for damp terrain & hard climbing get a good pair of boots. They should be a little big so they don't rub your toes going downhill and they have to be big enough for 2 pairs of socks over swollen feet. If you plan to do a lot of hiking have them custom built. They must support your ankles, but shouldn't go much above. Leather boots with soles of cork or rubber lug, lowheeled, and well broken in, light weight and durable are best. Wax or grease your boots every once in in a while to preserve the leather

Most common troubles: blisters puncture edge of blister with a sterile needle, press out fluid, apply antiseptic, gauze, and tape. Sprains. leave the shoe on. Place bandage or bandana under instep. Cross ends behind heel and again over arch and tie under foot in a tight square knot. mountain sickness (headache nausea & fatigue): prevent by being fully acclimated before hiking, eating a substantial breakfast but a light lunch, and don't drink water, just rinse your mouth when necessary. (see also "ticks" under "troublesome neighbors"; and "frostbite" under "first aid")

food to carry on trail: dried fruit (quick energy, also if it has a pit you can suck it for hours, which keeps your mouth from going dry), nuts (light weight source of concentrated fat & protein), raw fruits & vegetables & sandwiches. For extended camping trips, dried whole grains, roasted soybeans (take too long to cook if raw), dried milk powder (you can make yogurt in a thermos jug — heat milk in morning, carry all day in pack, by evening you have a thermos of yogurt — be sure you bring a spoonful of already cultured yogurt to start it), instant soup — just add boiling water & cut up wild greens if you have any: miso or soy sauce, brewer's yeast, dried parsley, paprika, cumin, instant onion flakes, dried kelp (kombu), and you can boil up separately some noodles to put in. sprouts are also easy to do in a pack (see "sprouts"). Breakfast cereal — (see "muesli"). Jerky (see "meat") — flour & sourdough culture (* see "sourdough") salted fish (see "fish"). dried vegetables for soup or stews (see "drying") nut butters (can even be used as soup base) honey (quick energy), flat bread or crackers (see "quick breads").

8

bed of boughs: prepare
space as below. Thatch
with pine boughs starting
at head, needles toward
head, sticks pointing
down, then reinforce
with boughs
woven in
sideways.

camp on a level
space. Smooth the area
of rocks & sticks; dig a trough
at shoulder and hip levels. Test out
your space. Then spread your ground
cloth, pitch your tent, put down your bag. If you use an
air mattress it should be slightly underinflated. A foam
rubber mountain climbers mattress is light & not too expensive;
goes from top of head to under hips. Tent opening should face
away from wind. Bring in equipment to protect from dew.

water: When looking for water in the woods, look for low grooves & ravines with lush green especially with willow trees. at the sea coast, dig a hole below the high tide mark at the time of low tide. Fresh water is lighter than salt water and floats on top. The water that seeps into your hole should be fresh. If it is not, don't drink it; salt water only increases one's thirst. One way to get water is to lay out a big piece of canvas or plastic overnight; dew will collect in the lowest part. Large leaves & rock basins will also collect water.

Purification: add a drop of iodine to a container of water. Drink it after 30 minutes (time for iodine to work). or add 1 tablespoon alum to 4 gallons of water and allow several days for impurities to settle. To sweeten water, boil it, with some hardwood charcoal and strain through fine cloth.

10

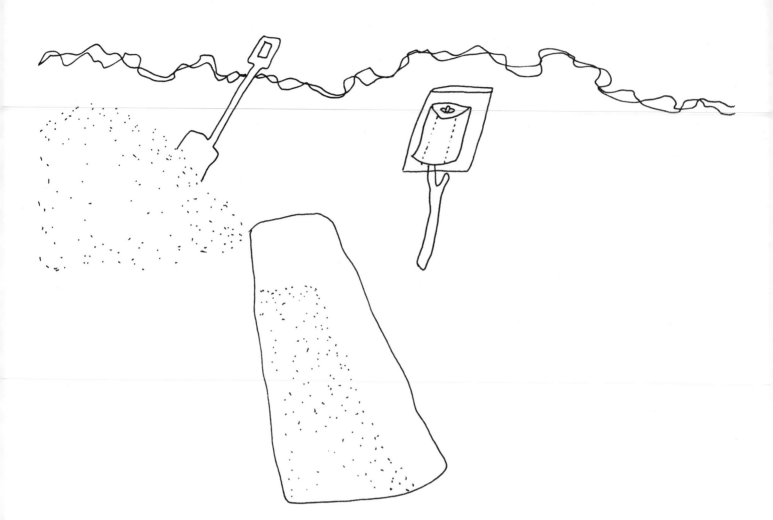

a proper shit-hole: site must not be above water supply.

dig a trench about three feet deep, one foot wide and three feet long. as you shit, cover it with the dirt from the hole. Toilet paper can be placed on a stick with a plastic bag over it to keep it dry. Or put it in a coffee can.

If your hole is on a slanted area, make sure you make the trench pointing up and down rather than sideways. If it is sideways you will squat over it with all your weight on one leg.

Dig it far enough away from your camp so you won't be bothered with flies.

Tent of Three Blankets

first: dig four holes for the poles. the poles should
be six feet or more and of equal length. Bury
them two feet deep. Space them two inches
closer together than the corners of the biggest
blanket.

then: stretch the biggest blanket across the four poles
and tie the corners onto the tops of the poles thus:

tie with a half hitch and a square knot

now: add each of the other two blankets.
secure 2 corners of one side to 2
of the poles. then place a smooth stone
half-way between the poles under the
margin of overlap and tie a knot
around it from the top. Drive 2
stakes into the ground at each end.
tie stones to the corners of the blankets
and tie each corner tautly to a stake (see drawing).

12

2 blanket pack:

pack all small items inside one blanket

tie pack with rope:  ↑add straps

roll up the other blanket:

and attach it:

bring straps over shoulders, cross in front and
tie to pack

how to pan gold

gold pans are sold in most sierra towns. blacken the
pan so the gold will contrast. Look for crevices with black
sand and dig it out with a spoon. Place sand in pan
and rotate the pan in shallow water. The gold,
which is heavier than the sand, will fall to the
bottom. Remove the gold with tweezers and store
it in a little bottle.

Another method is to dive wearing a face
mask and pry up underwater rocks with
a crowbar.

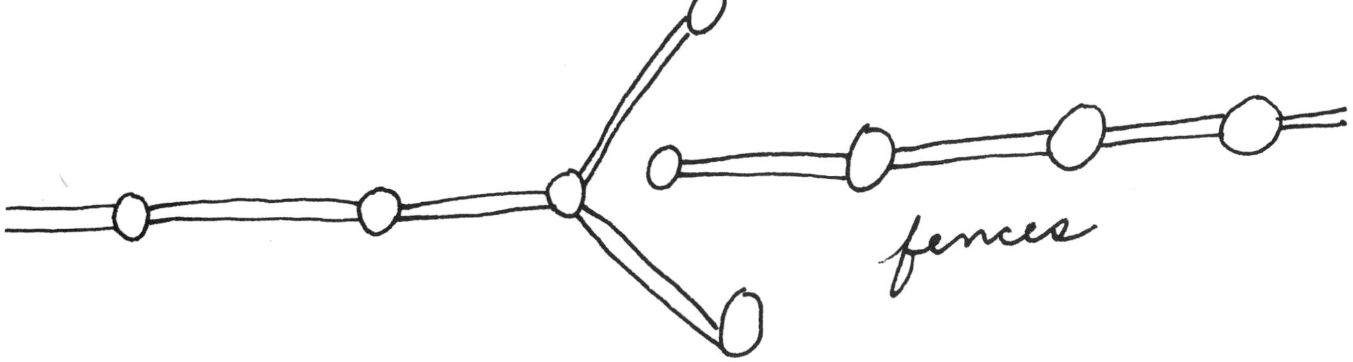

fences

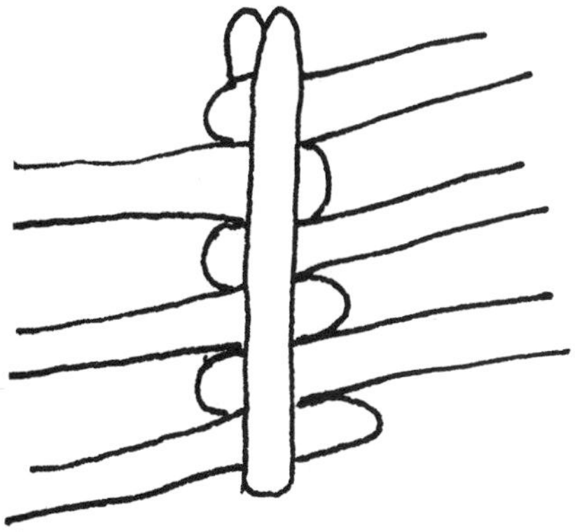

one simple fence: every 6 feet
drive 2 posts into the ground
as far apart as your fence
beams are wide. Stack up the
beams as shown at right.

gate to cattle pasture (above): a man
can easily slip in and out the opening
but an animal with a long barrel —
horse or cow — cannot. The circles
are posts and the lines are beams.

garden fence: dig a ditch around garden and
set up posts in ditch. Then put on the
chicken wire and fill in the ditch. An
underground fence keeps out gophers. 14

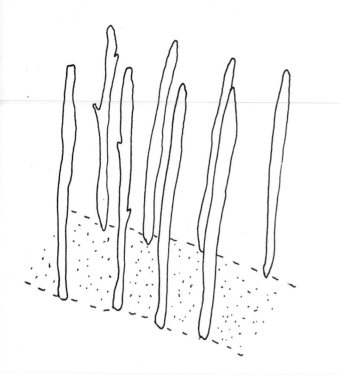

shelter . . .

clear and make level a floor space. dig holes 2 feet deep along the sides and insert tall poles. choose a site out of wind and possible falling trees.

bend poles to meet as arches. lash them together. lash one long pole along the top of all the arches and additional poles along the sides.

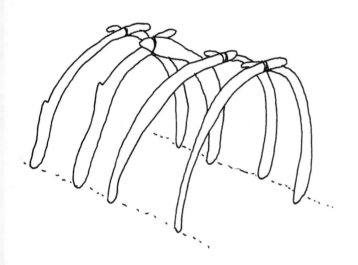

cover with a tarp or some plastic or an old tent or even a blanket.

turn the cover under the Bottom transverse pole (which is lashed to the outside of the frame) and sew it together.

if rain is imminent: cover with plastic with 2 feet extra on the sides. Dig a ditch around shelter and bury extra plastic so rain will run off top and into ditches.

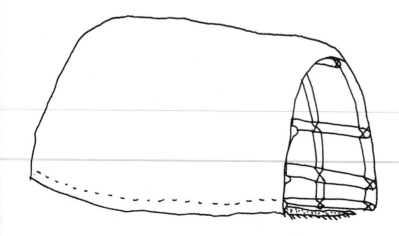

a dome for all weather

site: preferably where no trees can fall on it and with no
slopes above it so water can't run in during rain.
dig a ditch around circular cleared area if you are
below a slope.

frame: dig holes for the branches. lash at top. Brace
against wind with diagonal branches. Tie strips
of cardboard on tops of branches to protect the plastic.

door: face away from prevailing winds but east is best
for seeing the sunrise from your bed.

walls: cover frame except where door goes and leave a space
at top for a skylight. any cloth will do. Behind
the stove put a sheet of metal. For cold weather
add insulation (fiberglass) over the cloth.
Cover with clean plastic. Bury edges all around dome.
Caution: plastic is very flammable.

16

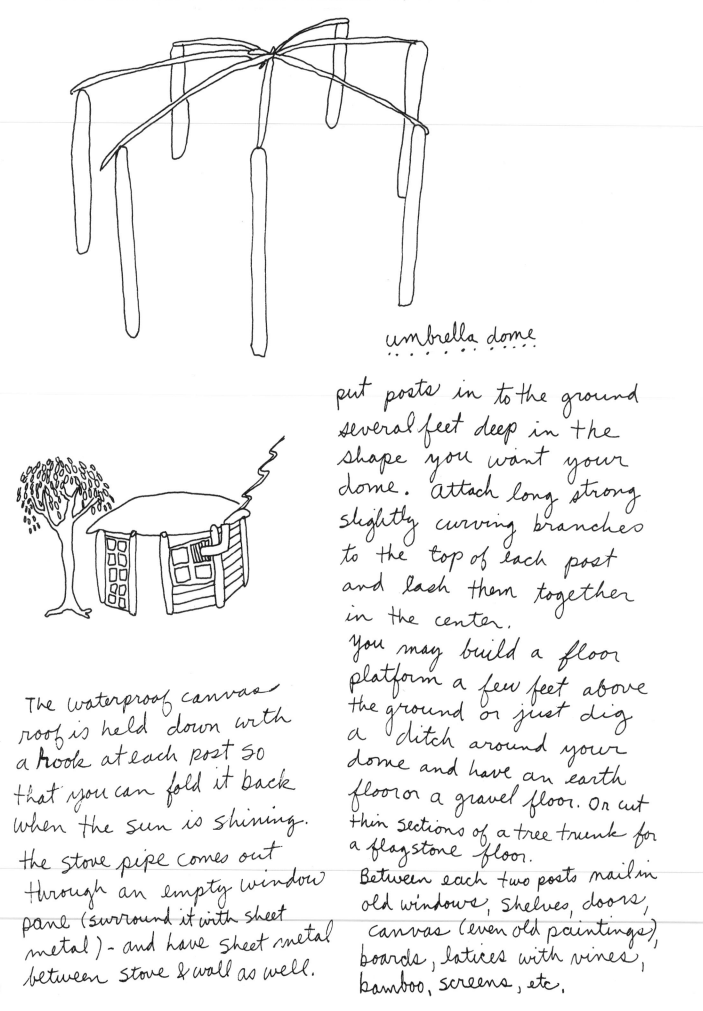

umbrella dome

put posts in to the ground several feet deep in the shape you want your dome. attach long strong slightly curving branches to the top of each post and lash them together in the center.

you may build a floor platform a few feet above the ground or just dig a ditch around your dome and have an earth floor or a gravel floor. Or cut thin sections of a tree trunk for a flagstone floor.

Between each two posts nail in old windows, shelves, doors, canvas (even old paintings), boards, latices with vines, bamboo, screens, etc.

The waterproof canvas roof is held down with a hook at each post so that you can fold it back when the sun is shining. the stove pipe comes out through an empty window pane (surround it with sheet metal) - and have sheet metal between stove & wall as well.

17

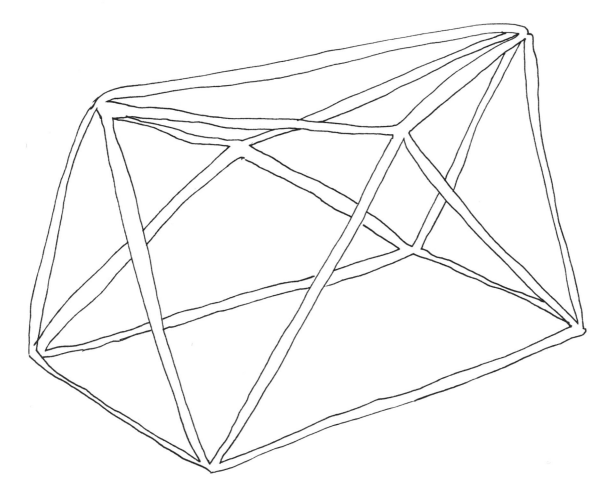

the triangle house can be altered into innumerable
complex shapes. above is the basic design: an opposing
pair of tall triangles, an opposing pair of short triangles,
and the two tallest points connecting to form the height
of the ceiling. It uses space more economically than an
A-frame. a twelve-sided house would have two
tall triangles and ten smaller ones. The frame can be
covered with cloth painted many coats, or plastic,
or canvas. the width and length can be varied, and
other rooms can be connected by sharing one triangle
between them. cheap lumber: buy from a wrecker or
work as a wrecker yourself, lumber mill-ends, lumber
seconds (the boards that have bark on one side).

18

if you live on land that has been raped ("logged")
you may find stumps that work as
foundations for your house. Sometimes
a large redwood is cut down but the little
ones around it are left, forming a little
pavillion. However, do not put nails in living
trees: many times it kills them. The little pipe
is the sink drain (can go right into the garden if
you use biodegradable soap). Roof: sealing with melted
tar or polyurethane works better than roofing paper.

archologies

paolo soleri, an architect who designs cities of the future based on organic forms which allow as much as possible a harmonious relationship with the local ecology, has a community in scottsdale, arizona. The buildings there are formed of cement poured over forms made by piling up mounds of earth (for a dome shape) and digging them out from underneath! The pillars & arches (poured in plywood forms) take a crane to lift them into position, but they certainly can be incredible to look at. and they can be decorated by pressing things into the forms (lumber, bottles etc.) that leave an imprint.

mobile homes

above — a mattress thrown in the back of a
     pick-up truck. a sheet of plastic
     can be thrown over the bars in case
     of foul weather. a simple summer
     home with a good motor. (and a view).

the ritz — a bus (school or VW) or a milk
     or mail van. a skylight of plexiglass
     helps. hammocks are "fold-away beds".
     fishnet wall pockets keep things
     visible & unbroken (maybe).

what to take......

tools:

carpentry tools
gardening tools
chain saw
axe & hatchet
knives (a buck
or scout knife
should be very sharp
so sharpen it every
day and don't ever
use it on any metal)
wire & wirecutters
mortar & pestle
kitchen tools: cast iron
pots & pans, crocks,
canning equipment,
baking pans, dishes,
plastic containers, new
clean garbage cans (for
storage), woodstove,
kerosene lamps, flint &
steel (to light fires), grinder,
barrels, washtub, broom,
dishpans, scrubboard,
metal racks.
camping tools: compass,
binoculars, tents,
backpacks, buckets.

supplies:

first aid kit

bedding: sleeping
bags, blankets, cloth,
foam rubber mattresses.

books & art supplies

musical instruments

building materials: plastic
sheets, parachutes, canvas,
paint, pipe, insulation,
rope, nails, screws.

dry goods: towels, pencils
can openers, steel wool.

food: dried grains & beans
        any special supplements.
garden: seeds, fruit trees, fencing.
miscellaneous: matches, wax,
kerosene, string, tacks,
cheesecloth, alum, soda,
biodegradable soap, paraffin,
fish hooks, lots of tightly
closing waterproof containers,
sewing supplies, sponges
animals: poultry, cow or goats,
cat for rodents, pack animals.

a houseboat should be streamlined to offer the least resistance to wind & tide. Lots of windows, lots of deck space (on both ends), some growing things, some hanging things (hammock), a fire place, a sleeping loft, a flock of ducks, maybe even a sunken bathtub in front of the fire place (covered with a hatch and a rug when not in use). Drains on sinks just go straight out.
So do organic wastes, except what you can burn. Glass & metal should be disposed of on shore. A watertight box may be lowered into the water as a cooler for food.

Some practical aspects to consider: The bilge pump, stove, refrigeration, toilet (a bucket re-filled with water after dumping overside), storage for drinking water, gas, firewood, clothes, food, books, etc. Shelves need railings to keep things from falling in storm, tables & counters can fold into the wall.

houseboats can be built on all kinds of floating things: a boat hull, a landing craft, a barge (above), styrofoam floats, a raft of sealed oil drums, or ferro cement hollow floats. The latter need the least care although the initial expense is the greatest. Styrofoam & oil drums don't offer maneuverability but they are cheap. A nautical craft requires that you pump water out of the bilge every few days, but it maneuvers well both in storm & in travel. Wooden crafts must be scraped & repainted every 2 or 3 years. Cheap flotation often needs replacement. In any case you will need rope, an anchor, a rowboat, night lights, and maybe a motor. 24

furniture

barrels can be
modified into chairs,
rocking cradles,
even cabinets.

a simple bench (build
it with a backward tilt
to the back) can be
covered with long pillows
and makes a comfortable
sofa.

a girl named dana
at gate 5 sausalito
designed this chair →
It is 2 identical
plywood forms: L
and a number of little
1" X ½" boards of identical
length. after nailing the
boards to the 2 forms, you
might stain it dark
and varnish it.

build a kayak...

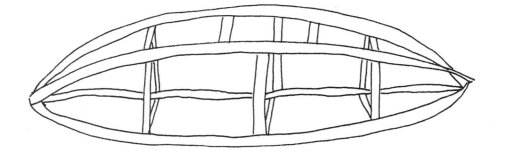

you will need 5 pieces of flexible wood (yellow pine, redwood, etc.) equal in length (about 8 to 16 feet long) 1 inch by 1 inch. Also some short pieces for braces and a pole 6 or 8 feet long and some boards for the paddle.

1. nail together at each end 2 of the pieces. Pull apart like a bow and insert a brace of the width you want your kayak. (not under 30 inches) add 2 smaller braces: ⬭. This is the bottom section.

2. Do top section same way except use 2 braces to form the front & back of cockpit, and 2 smaller braces: ⬭

3. Attach top and bottom sections at ends and add braces to determine height of kayak. (above)

4. Nail strip along middle of bottom for keel. Cover with cloth and paint with many coats of paint.

5. paddle: a long pole with a thin board at each end:

26

button stone hammock: fold
six inches of the end of a
blanket over a strong stick. Place
a small round stone under the
2 layers and tie a knot around
the knob made by the stone
through the 2 layers. make
several of these knobs at each
end and tie a rope to each end
of each stick to hang it up (above).

macramé hammock: drive a row of nails into
a long board and tie a long piece of heavy string
or cord to each nail A. Divide the strings into pairs
and loop each of the strings in each pair around the
other B. leaving the first string free, divide the
strings into pairs again and loop them C. Then
loop original pairs continuing until
strings are all used. Knot the ends of each
string to itself after looping them around
two metal rings D. Hang the rings with rope.

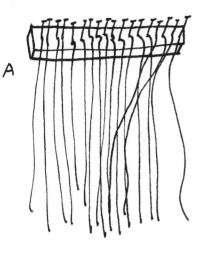

A

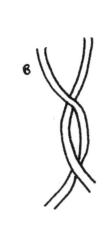

B

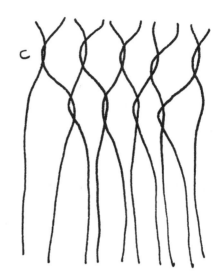

C

D

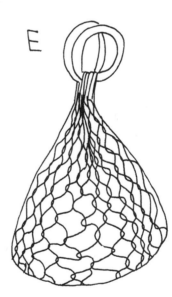

E

By looping together each side (after folding in half so that the metal rings are together) you can make a bag. E

29

beaded curtains: make a soupy paste of flour & water. Take a long string and tack it so it is horizontal (easier to work). Dip strips of newspaper in the "soup" and wind them around the string at intervals forming a row of beads. When dry, paint the beads, and finish with shellac or clear **wood** varnish.

a touch of fantasy - when you build your own nest it reflects you. (All my nests have had a dream-like quality) any old floor (if the wood isn't pretty to look at) can be covered with plywood, painted with enamels in a fanciful way, and given a coat of polyurethane (liquid plastic) which, when it seals, is easy to clean & very durable. (Polyurethane is also great for table tops and other woodwork - dries clear and gives a washable surface). Mosaic tiles are simply flat pieces of glazed clay. A wall, a counter top, a fountain are beautiful covered with tile. The Simon Rodia towers in Watts (Los Angeles) are inspirational mosaic. Rodia used bits of plates, pop bottles & Spanish tile to create his compositions.

the kitchen area ...

the kitchen is the center of the home. the fire is the center of the kitchen. a fire should be enclosed, especially in summer when fires start easily in the forest. the best year-round woodstove is a cast iron stove. If you move often, the best is a drum — a fifty-five gallon drum (with a kit that turns it into a stove. which you can get from army surplus.) When you move, take the kit and get a new drum the next place you move. It makes a big hot stove. If you prefer a gas camping stove — if you are backpacking you will — get a one-burner. a two-burner requires unnecessary hassle. Some simple enclosed woodfires: Build fire in a garbage can, or push together a few cement bricks to resemble a chimney (on cleared flat ground.) or dig a pit and line it with rocks that don't come from a streambed or tidepool. (These explode.) a metal bread box can be used as an oven. Keep a wood-box supplied with kindling and wood.

the kitchen...
continued

when you're living outdoors, all food should be stored in plastic, glass, or metal containers, so insects and other animals won't bother it. The best storage bin is a clean brand new metal trash can with a tight lid. Hot dog stands often sell or give away one gallon plastic containers (which they use for salad dressings.) These, cleaned and dried in the sun, make good flour & sugar containers. Empty coffee cans and cookie tins and glass jars work well for smaller things.

Shelves are easily constructed of boards, bricks or cement blocks, and crates. You will need a wooden cutting board and a knife, a collander, and some kind of refrigeration for vegetables (see "refrigeration"). The best kind of pots and frying pans are heavy cast iron. You will need a spatula, a ladle, a stirring spoon (can be wooden) and plates, cups, and chopsticks or silverware. An easy sink is a bowl, elevated, with a hole in the bottom and a place for the hole to drain. Use plastic jugs for water supply. Grow your own herbs in pots!

the woodstove

A damper
B slide damper
C fire box
D lower grate
E oven
F range top
G warming oven

clean the stove before starting a fire (stove is cold). Take out half-burned wood - save for next fire, sweep ashes into the lower grate and into a metal pail. Use ashes in compost or soap. rub on a little stove polish. Rub in polish as the stove heats.

to start a fire open both dampers, crumple newspaper or pile up wood shavings. lay thin wood strips across the tops and light. add more pieces of soft wood as blaze grows. when you have a good layer of red coals & fire, start adding hardwood. Close slide vent. Control fire with damper (A).

oven temperature sprinkle a little flour on a pie tin and place in oven. Wait 30 seconds. If it browns before 30, the oven is too hot for baking (leave door open awhile) If flour just begins to tan at 30 it is just right, put in your bread.

to remove rust from stove sandpaper it and rub with oil. to rustproof: melt 3 parts lard to 1 part resin. apply thin coat.

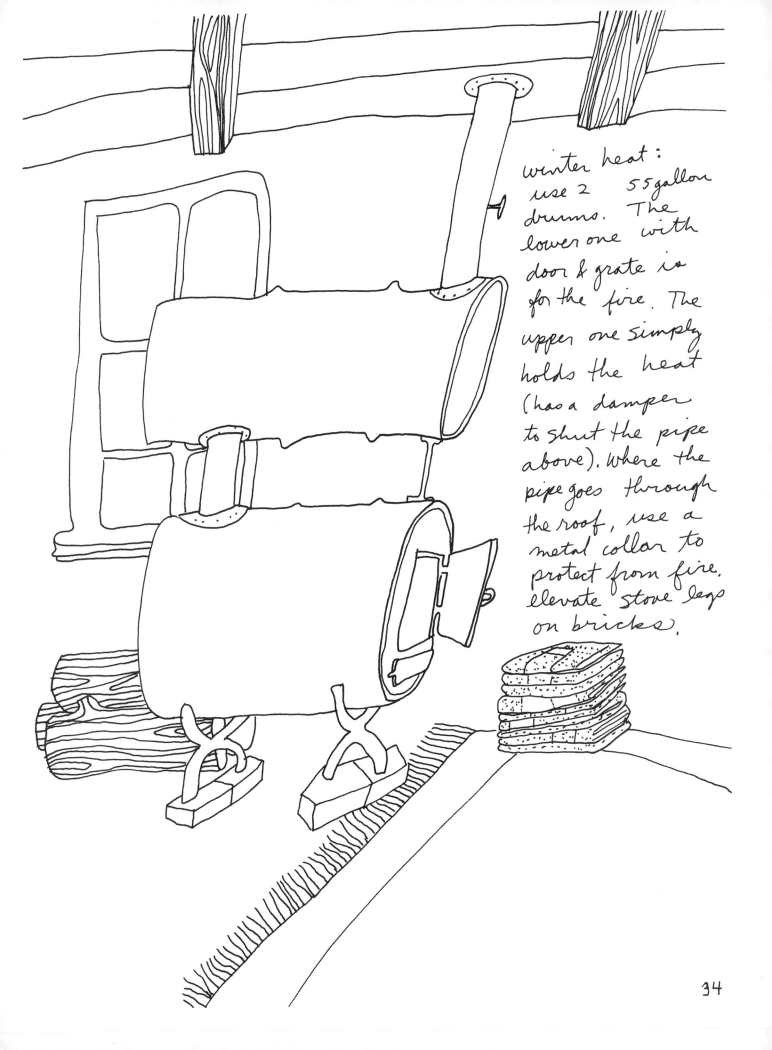

winter heat:
use 2   55 gallon
drums. The
lower one with
door & grate is
for the fire. The
upper one simply
holds the heat
(has a damper
to shut the pipe
above). where the
pipe goes through
the roof, use a
metal collar to
protect from fire.
elevate stove legs
on bricks.

34

another cooler is a large pot in a shady place. Fill ⅓ full with cold water and place another pot inside. Put food in inner pot, place lid on, and cover large pot. (see also "Ice chest")

spring house: build a shelter to shade your spring and to keep out animals. Place containers of food in a wire basket in the cold flowing water.

REFRIGERATION

Put food in a wet canvas bag. Leave bag in the sun & keep it wet at all times. The evaporation keeps the food cold.

In a shady spot dig a hole and line it with sticks. cover the floor with flat stones. Make a cover by lashing together a frame of sticks and weaving long grasses through it. Closed containers and uncut fruit will keep cool in a stream.

If you are visited by animals — hang your refrigerator from a tree: Cover a crate with burlap and hang the crate from a limb in the shade. Keep the burlap wet. Keep all food in containers to keep out insects. To repel bugs — leave an open container of vinegar with food.

how to build an ice chest: get or build two boxes, one a few inches bigger in each dimension than the other. Line the smaller one with "contac" paper or oil cloth. Fill the larger box with a few inches of sawdust so that the tops of the boxes are level when one is placed inside the other. Pack more saw-dust around the four sides of the small box and add wood strips to hold it in place. bore a hole through bottom of chest, insert drain pipe. make a lid that covers and loosely nail some vinyl inside, with more sawdust behind it.

an ice chest
· · · · · ·   · · · · · ·
if ice is available to you, but not gas or electricity, this is one means of refrig-eration. Be sure to place a bucket underneath to catch the water as the ice melts. you should make the inside surfaces slick for easy cleaning (which should be done weekly). 36

doing laundry
by hand:

1. Separate into piles: delicate things, white things, bright colored things, very soiled things, and heavy things (like blankets).

2. assemble:
1 large tub or barrel to rinse in
2 other tubs to wash in
a washboard
clothes line & clothespin
2 large baskets
a wagon or baby carriage helps for moving things around

a pail and ladle

soap: if you use biodegradable soap, like: basic H" or the detergent sold at the Co-op markets, the laundry water can be used beneficially to water the garden.

first wash the delicate things: fill one tub ⅓ full of warm water, add a little soap. Don't use the washboard. Press out soapy water gently; don't wring. Rinse in clear water, hang up to dry.

then the white things: more vigorously. for coarser & dirtier things use the wash board. Don't rinse yet.

Place washed clothes in the other tub. Pour over some boiling water & soap. Stir with a stick. Drain in a basket, place clean cold water in first tub and rinse drained clothes in it.

Wool & man-made fabrics like nylon, acetate, orlon, etc. should be washed as delicate items but should be rinsed in hot water and placed on towels to dry. Stretch them to their original dimensions as you place them on the towel.

Hanging up the wash: if the weather is windy or frosty, leave the clothes in rinse water until fair weather; otherwise the clothes will be worn and damaged.

Wring each thing around a pole, then shake out to its original shape before hanging it up.

Spots: blood stains come out easier with cold water than hot. Coffee stains & fruit stains: pour boiling water onto stretched cloth from a height of 2 feet.

Velvet: to smooth crushed velvet, hold it over steam, pile side up; then pass it over the edge of a hot iron, pile side up.

FATS: use soft fats (poultry & vegetable) with hard fats (beef & mutton) for better texture. The finest soaps are all vegetable.

castile soap: use vegetable oil: coconut, cottonseed, palm, soy, etc. in the same proportions (by weight) as fats.

Raw fat: chop fine and cook over moderate heat with 1 quart water per 10 pounds raw fat. Stir. when cracklings settle, strain.

meat drippings: bring to a boil and remove from heat: equal parts drippings and water. Cool; add one quart cold water per gallon of hot liquid. Skim fat off the surface. The salt and other impurities are at bottom.

rancid fat: Boil in a solution of 1 part vinegar to 5 parts water. cool and skim off fat. Remelt fat and add 1 quart cold water per gallon hot fat. Stir, cool, and skim fat off top.

how to make soap

LYE: Sodium hydroxide content 85 to 98% (check label on can) (or follow directions to make lye) one 13 ounce can of lye is enough for 6 pounds of fat. always have a bowl of vinegar handy to dunk hands in if any lye gets on them. Drink vinegar if lye is swallowed. lye is a heavy poison. it burns.

AND: you may add these
borax (for quick suds)
coconut oil (for a fine soap)
fragrant oils - like oil of lemon or oil of sassafras (perfumed soap)
oil of tar (for tar soap & hampoo)
pumice stone powder & castor oil (for mechanic's hand soap)

EQUIPMENT: 2 bowls - earthenware or heat-proof glass don't use aluminum. one 2 quart bowl and one 6 quart bowl with a round bottom
one wooden slotted spoon
a dairy thermometer
a houshold scale
measuring cups & spoons
mold: a flat wooden box soaked in water and lined with a wet cotton cloth.

39

(continued next page)

proportions

6 pounds of fat
1 can of lye (13 ounces)
5 cups cold soft water
(use 7 cups with beef or mutton tallow)

temperature of ingredients

type of fat	temp: melted fat	temp: lye solution
tallow	120°-130°F	90°-95°F
lard and tallow (equal)	100°-110°F	80°-85°F
soft fresh lard or fat	80°-85°F	70°-75°F
soft rancid lard or fat	97°-100°F	75°-80°F

method

1. slowly pour lye into cold water and stir to dissolve in the 2 quart bowl. cool to temperature in chart.

2. put melted fat (correct temperature) in 6 quart bowl. add lye in a slow steady stream. Stir slowly until mixture is thick and creamy.

3. you may make floating soap by folding in some air. or you may add 2 tablespoons of borax, 1 or 2 tablespoons of fragrant oils, 8 ounces of oil of tar, or 6 ounces of coconut oil (for above proportions).

4. pour into the wet mold. when set, cut into cakes and pile so that air circulates around each cake. age soap one month before using. don't allow new soap to freeze.

5. for granular soap just leave it in the bowl a few hours until it becomes crumbly and store it in a cardboard box.

mechanic's hand soap

over a moderate heat, dissolve 3 pounds homemade soap in 6 cups water and add 1 tablespoon borax and 3 ounces of light mineral oil. when cooled to a creamy consistency work in 5 pounds of pumice stone powder and pour into wet mold.

if the soap separates

soap should be neutral. If excess lye is used, the soap "bites" when it touches your tongue. Don't touch soap that has separated. Chop it up and reboil it with 2/3 pint water per pound of soap. Wear gloves, and be careful — it boils over easily. boil until the mixture drops from a spoon in sheets. Pour into mold.

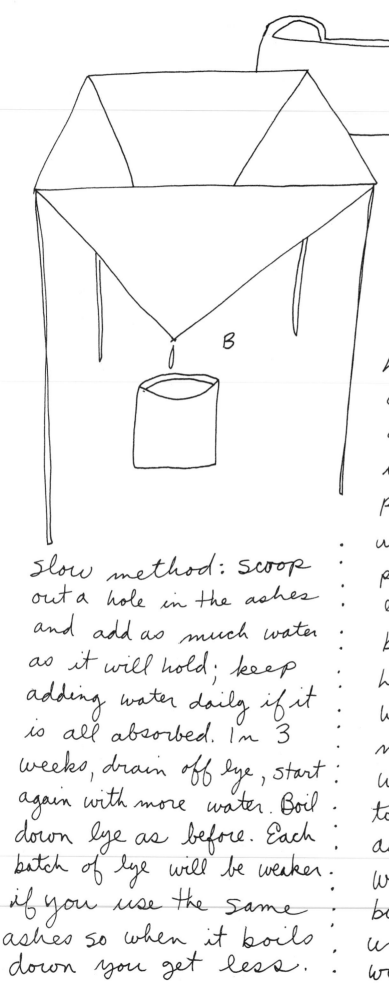

A

B

more about soap
....

home-made lye: either open the side of a barrel and place a spigot on it (A) or build a pyramid-shaped box (B) with an opening at the point. Elevate high enough to put a large bucket underneath. Line with straw. Fill with wood ashes. Fast method: sprinkle enough water on some quick-lime to crumble it. Place over ashes and add hot water. When it drains into bucket, boil down lye until a raw potato won't sink in it.

slow method: scoop out a hole in the ashes and add as much water as it will hold; keep adding water daily if it is all absorbed. In 3 weeks, drain off lye, start again with more water. Boil down lye as before. Each batch of lye will be weaker if you use the same ashes so when it boils down you get less.

using paraffin

always have a lid handy to cover a pot of melting paraffin as it is flammable.

how to waterproof canvas: dissolve paraffin in kerosene (as much as you can melt in) and paint it on canvas with a paint brush. However, this makes canvas flammable.

instant canned heat: cut a strip of cardboard one inch wide and about a yard long and roll it into a tight spiral and place in an empty tuna fish can. Pour melted paraffin over and let it set. It burns a long time.

instant campfire: tear newspaper into strips 3 inches wide. Roll up tightly into little "logs" an inch in diameter. Secure with string. Dip in melted paraffin and dry. Store in a plastic bag. Two will kindle a fire.

household chemistry:

rustproofing — melt 3 parts lard to 1 part resin & apply in a thick coat.

shoe polish — equal parts oil, vinegar & molasses. add enough lamp black to form a paste. apply to shoes with a flannel rag.

lamp black — place a funnel over a kerosene lamp and from the funnel run a pipe out of the room so the smoke can escape. a black oily light substance will form on the walls of the funnel. scrape it out with a sharp surface. (see picture)

water proofing — boil 2½ pounds alum in 10 gallons of water and either paint this on to cloth or allow the cloth soaking time. Rinse in cold water. For rain-coats, ground cloths, etc., dissolve 5 pounds india rubber by boiling it in 1 gallon boiled linseed oil and paint this onto cloth.

varnish — place in a jar ½ pound gum shellac and 1/5 gallon alcohol. leave in a warm place to dissolve.

paint remover — 1 part turpentine to 2 parts ammonia

43

waterproofing for leather — melt 1 cup tallow over a low fire with 1/4 cup beeswax. Blend in 1/2 cup castor oil. Cool & apply

glue — heat up shellac in a metal vessel. Take to a safe open place & set it afire. When the alcohol burns off you have glue, which you should use immediately or else store in a bottle with 1 part whiskey to 2 parts glue until needed.

alum — is difficult to make, but one can buy it. It has manifold uses: as a mordant agent for dyes, sets hair into furs, hardens candles, waterproofs cloth, hardens pickles, purifies water. Its chemical name is Sodium aluminum sulphate $(NaAl(SO_4)_2)$.

baking soda — (sodium bicarbonate) extinguishes fires, makes breads rise, is a dentifrice, is soothing added to bath water and is used in various medical ways.

making lampblack

44

Household Recipes....

root cellar: dig a large hole & line with straw 6 inches thick all around so that a large barrel will sit in it. Fill barrel with harvested roots, squashes or individually wrapped, perfect apples & pears. The hole may be lined with plastic sheet before adding straw to insure dry storage. Cover barrel with lid, then more straw, then a layer of plastic, then dirt.

scouring pad: the bottle brush-like horse-tail plant is rich in silicon and scours well. It is found growing in wet places. Sand from a stream bed will scour more adamant spots.

broom: the branches of the scottish broom plant (check naturalist's book for illustrative description) can be bound to a stick and used to sweep with.

air freshner: vinegar set out in an open dish absorbs the odor of smoke.

greasy pots: wipe first with newspaper, then scrub with cornmeal (raw). soak pots after using so that food won't harden before you wash them.

squeaky doors &
sticking drawers: rub joints with soap.

lantern for candles: open a can on the side
with an I shaped
cut; make 2 holes
at top to attach a
wire handle.

or just place the candle in
a glass jar and place
a cylinder of paper around
it to diffuse it (a soft table
light). don't let flame touch jar.

protect kitchen walls: hang up a piece of sandpaper
to strike matches on.

cleaning pots: to remove rust from cast iron
pots, clean dairy equipment, &
sweeten a sour-tasting pot,
boil water and some clean hay in
pot, let stand overnight, and boil
again with clean water.

the griddle: pancakes won't stick if you rub griddle
with salt before using.

straw mats: to clean - dissolve 1 cup salt in
1 quart water. wash a small area
at a time with this and dry at
once before going on to next area.

how to deal with troublesome neighbors   Part 1.

Rats ...... place powdered potash or liquid chloride of lime near their holes. They will move away. Caution: keep these chemicals away from people & pets

cockroaches .... mix ½ borax and ½ brown sugar, place a dish of this where they travel.

flies .... keep your compost heap well covered. If flies congregate, leave them a dish of molasses & black pepper.

most flying bugs... hate smoke; light a stick of incense. crawling bugs... will leave when 3 quarts boiled water with 2 pounds alum is painted on walls and cracks.

fleas ...... flea collar: soak a string in oil of pennyroyal (an herb). Change collar every 2 weeks. also bunches of the herb may be hung in dog house. a pillow of camomile flowers will drive them away.

mosquitoes will also avoid the smell of pennyroyal. Rub the oil on your skin or put sachets of the herb with your clothes. a purple martin (bird) can eat 1000 mosquitoes per day. Build a martin a home. Mosquitoes like wet clothes and the color blue.

moths

a chest built of cedarwood is mothproof. any other chest, painted several coats inside and out with oil of cedar, will be mothproof. Sachets of cedarwood chips should be placed with woollens & furs in storage. To get moths to leave the room, darken the room and set a bright light outside. They will fly to it.

Bees and their relatives

most bees won't bother a calm human. they will be induced to leave a room as moths are. If bees are numerous and attacking people (yellow jackets and hornets will), place a glass jar or jug (with a small opening) outside your house with water in the bottom and honey or fruit juice on the rim and inside. It will fill with drowned bees.

ticks

a tick is about 1/8 inch long, dark red brown, and is seen mostly in spring and early summer. It bites in like a corkscrew, puffs up with blood. It may carry tick fever on its body; don't touch it if you can avoid it. get it to back out by applying a hot needle or alcohol to its rear end. If you can't do it that way, "unscrew" it gently counter clockwise (otherwise the head will remain in the skin) and sterilize skin and fingers.

ants:

boil 1 pint tar in 2 quarts water and leave in an open dish where ants go. red ants hate sea sand & oyster shells. Small black ants hate sprigs of wormwood (herb)

insects & spiders

all flee from a cotton wad soaked in oil of pennyroyal. Fleas & mosquitoes hate the taste of vitamin B1. Take it orally.

48

Some things to consider about
communal living:

how many people do you want around?
on what basis will you select them?
how will you support yourselves?
how will you divide the responsibilities?
how will each person have privacy?
how will you all meet to share work,
    information & communication?
what is your transportation?
who, if anyone, is organizing things and
    what are his responsibilities?
how is your water supply? does it cover
    your needs?
how do your building & roads fit in
    with the local ecology?
what is your plan for garbage & sewage?
how will you deal with the government,
    with transient people, runaways, etc.?
will you need a school, an infirmary,
    meeting hall, community bathhouse?
what public health measures must you take?
what activities will be communal (cooking,
    gardening, building etc.)?

how will you educate your children?
how far away from cities do you want to be?
how many dogs will you allow?*
how will each person have time for himself
   as well as time to help the commune?
how will you divide the expenditures?
   *dogs bark, they chase & kill wildlife, they
   must be fed or they will be a nuisance (and hungry)

the free store

a shelter is allocated for all the things people aren't using and don't want around. Here one can look for what he needs, and share what he wants to share. Consider: Someone must keep the store in order. Someone must build the shelves & bins. This would be a good place for a community bulletin board.

the food co-op

if the commune buys food (or its members buy food — or other sundries — separately) the co-op helps avoid redundancy in trips to town. Simply have each member contribute (for example) 25¢ per week for gas and 2 hours per week of help (driving, shopping, measuring bulk quantities into individual orders, bookkeeping, etc.). The co-op takes orders for food from its members, buys in quantity certain items (saves money) and delivers (saves time).

sharing...

the San Francisco Diggers devised a way to make hundreds of loaves of whole grain bread in a day at a minimum of expense. Every slice was given away FREE.

you will need:
1. a very large oven
2. clean plastic trash cans for mixing and storing flour
3. a large flat surface for kneading.
4. coffee cans to bake bread in.
5. a sink to wash utensils
6. flour — go to railroad yards, docks, and damaged freight companies. Buy broken 100 pound bags.
7. yeast, salt, and oil.(See bread recipe)

Digger Bread

Step One - the night before baking: mix dry ingredients in the trash cans. Foam up yeast in warm milk or sugar water. Add yeast to flour and enough water to make a soft dough. Knead, cover and leave in a warm place overnight.

Step Two - the next morning: wash dry & grease the coffee cans. Knead dough; fill coffee cans half full of dough; let rise until cans are full. Bake, cool, remove loaves from cans and slice. 52

the sari is made of filmy cloth with a fancy design at one end. start with the plain end by tying together two handfuls of cloth at your waist.

bring the rest once around you and then throw the fancy end over your shoulder so it reaches your feet. Catch the rest in your other hand.

pleat the rest in front and tuck it in the front waist. Now take the fancy end off your shoulder.

bring the fancy end once more around your waist and throw it over your shoulder. This lady is playing finger cymbals.

53

hand sewing

the basic stitch of hand sewing is the "back stitch". First make a knot by taking one stitch and bringing the needle back through the loop you made (never knot the thread first.)

1. Now take one stitch forward:
2. go half-way back to the place your needle went in and take another stitch:
3. this stitch comes out ahead of the last. continue stitches that start behind & come out ahead:

1.

2.

3.

a row finished: - - - - - - - -
back side of cloth: ═══════════

TWO ANCIENT
& SIMPLE
ROBES

Bernoose:

measure length from shoulder
to ankle. use double that length
of cloth. width should be that
of hips or shoulders (widest
part) plus a few inches for
comfort. make a T shaped
slit for neck in center - trim
neck hole - and sew up sides
leaving arm holes. Tie at waist.

Draw string gown:

Take 2 identical sized pieces
of cloth and make a hem
at the top. The pieces should
to shoulder to ankle in length
and very wide for flow.
Sew sides together up to bottom
of arm holes. connect hems at
top and run a draw string or
elastic through to form gathered
neckline.

PILLOW

Step 1: cut a square piece of fabric.

Step 2: fold it over-right side in.

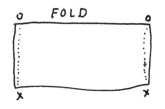

Step 3: Sew the sides up.

Step 4: Bring together seam ends from open side so that seam ends from the folded side form corners of pillow

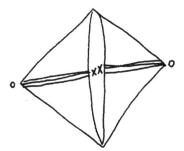

Step 5: Sew together opening leaving 6 to 8 inches open in the middle.

Step 6: Turn the pillow slip right side out

Step 7: Stuff it with foam rubber shreads or feathers or another pillow.

Step 8: Sew up central opening.

Step 9: Trim with tassles or a central button if you want.

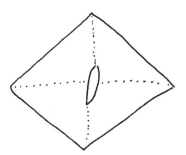

Making Your Own Patterns

Sleeves: measure the length you want (shoulder to wrist, elbow, etc.). add 2 inches for seams. measure around arm socket and add 2 inches for comfort.

On a large sheet of paper (newspaper is good), make the following:

Now take distance from shoulder to armpit and mark that on the "length" line. Draw the "armhole" line across at that point. Divide the armhole line in fourths. make the following:

the curve is the shape of top of sleeve.

if you want the sleeve to taper inward, measure the wrist plus 3 inches (you will have to make little pleats at the cuff unless you are using stretch material, in which case you can make the sleeve almost match the measurements of the arm.) if you want it to billow outward, measure how wide you want it and write that on:

cuffs: cut out 2 rectangles. the width: twice as wide as your cuffs should be long when finished (they'll be doubled over). length: the circumference of your wrist plus whatever space necessary to get your hands through (these cuffs have no buttons). Sew together the sides of each cuff and also the side seams of each sleeve. gather the sleeve hems to the cuffs, right side of cuff facing inside of sleeve. Fold over the cuff and sew to the outside of the sleeve, covering the first line you made

Making your own Patterns:

The body: measure as below and transfer to newspaper:

A shoulder to neck

B around the neck

C around arm socket

D neck to chest or bust

E bust or chest (widest part)

F length

G underarm to hem

H desired width at hem.

✷ if H is to be smaller than E, make darts so it will taper.

necklines can be any shape, but low ones in front will slide off at shoulders unless the neckline is high in the back.

trace ½ inch seam allowances all the way around.

darts: draw garment longer than needed and take a tuck where needed to add depth.

skirts: a gathered skirt is simple, just fold over the top of the cylinder (made by joining 2 sides of a rectangle of cloth) and adding a draw string or elastic.

if you prefer a belt, add it the same way you would add cuffs to a sleeve, except you must leave an opening for zipper or buttons

for an A-line skirt, cut out a shape as wide at the top as you are at the widest part of your hips and as wide at the bottom as you want the hem to be. Then keep making little tucks (darts) all around with pins until it fits you. Add a facing at the waist or a cuff if you intend to wear a belt with it.

you can make a djellava
from an army blanket.
you can leave off the hood
and shorten it to the
knees. you can make a
jacket by leaving an
opening in front (don't
sew cowl together).
   basic directions
. . . .
fold the cloth in
half and cut out
pieces according to
measurements
specified below.

a warm hooded robe

SLEEVES	HOOD
COWL	
BODY	

← FOLD

COWL: length is 2 or 3
      inches less than
      distance around
      shoulders, but be
      sure it fits over head.
BODY: distance from neck
      to ankle is length.
      any width.
SLEEVES: MEASURE armpit
         to wrist.
HOOD: any size

LINING: you can line it
        with an identical
        robe or an old shirt
61   with additions

method
. . . .

1. sew back seams on body, cowl, &
   sleeves. hood seam is back of head.
2. gather body to cowl leaving
   slits on sides for arm holes.
3. sew sleeves in slits
4. gather hood to cowl.
5. turn inside out & sew
   lining at seams

1. cut out the linings when you cut out the pieces of the garment. They should be exactly the same except the linings are made of a light weight fabric.

2. sew together the linings the same way you do the garment, except that all the seams should be on the outside instead of on the inside.

3. turn in the hems on the garment and turn in the cuffs and make facings as directed on next page.

4. place lining inside garment and attatch it to the garment at the shoulder points, the neck, under the arms, along the side seams and at the cuffs by sewing together the seam allowances for the garment & the lining.

5. turn under the edges of the facings ¼ inch and sew them to the linings using a hem stitch that won't show on the outside of the garment. Same with cuffs, but hems of garment & lining need not be attatched.

62

.facings...

1. finish garment except the outer edges (around neck or armholes) are still raw.

2. trace & cut out the shape of the neckline on a piece of paper and then cut a parallel line 3 inches out.

*also leave one inch of seam allowance where facings meet (at shoulders).

3. trace the paper cut-out onto cloth & cut out the shape in cloth.

4. place the cloth cut-out (facing) on the garment right sides facing.

be sure to sew together facings before placing on cloth

4 (cont'd) for example, sew together front & back neck facings at the shoulder seam allowance*

5. stitch facing to garment (garment is right side out, facing is back side up).

6. Turn the facing over so it's on the inside of the garment.

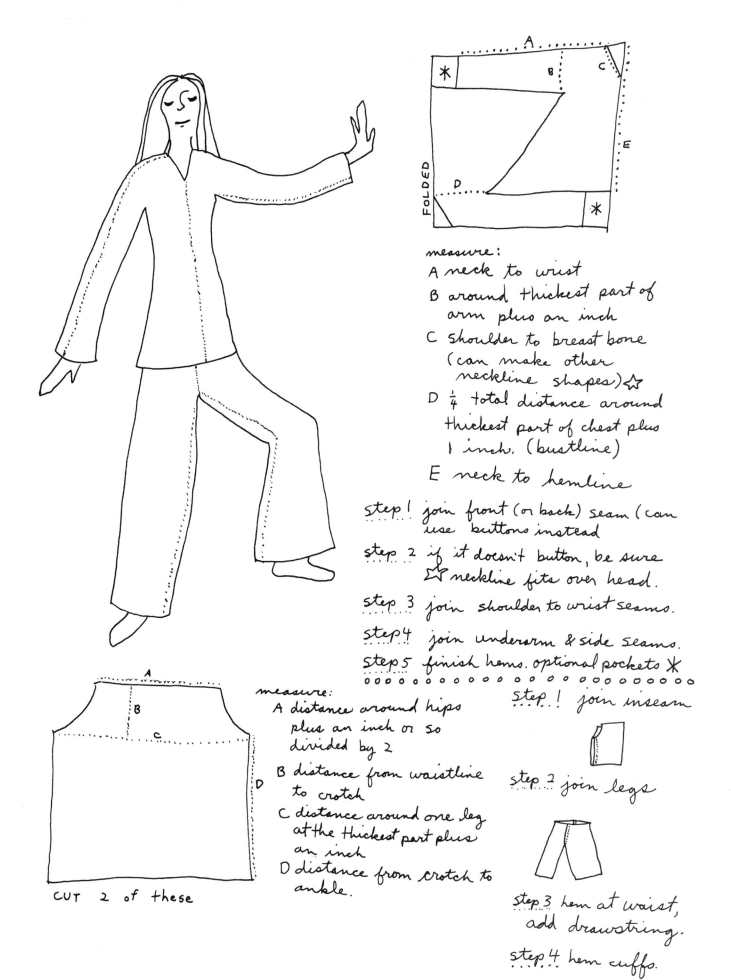

FOLDED

measure:

A neck to wrist

B around thickest part of arm plus an inch

C shoulder to breast bone (can make other neckline shapes) ☆

D ¼ total distance around thickest part of chest plus 1 inch. (bustline)

E neck to hemline

step 1 join front (or back) seam (can use buttons instead

step 2 if it doesn't button, be sure ☆ neckline fits over head.

step 3 join shoulder to wrist seams.

step 4 join underarm & side seams.

step 5 finish hems. optional pockets ✳

CUT 2 of these

measure:

A distance around hips plus an inch or so divided by 2

B distance from waistline to crotch

C distance around one leg at the thickest part plus an inch

D distance from crotch to ankle.

step 1 join inseam

step 2 join legs

step 3 hem at waist, add drawstring.

step 4 hem cuffs.

64

1. when the elastic is to be around the neck, make a facing (see facings).

2. when the elastic is to be at the wrists or ankles, make a cuff (just hem the edge 1 inch).

3. when the elastic is to be in the middle of a garment (waistline, under the bust, middle of a sleeve), cut out a strip of fabric 2 inches longer* than the garment's circumference at that place, and sew the strip to the garment along the inside. Then turn the strip over so that the seam allowance (from the first time you sewed it on) is under it. Make a ½ inch border (turned under) and sew it down to the garment. Leave 2 inches unsewn so you can put through elastic, then sew closed.

* the extra 2 inches is so you can sew the strip's ends together (with a 1 inch seam allowance) before you sew it to the garment.

4. to put in elastic: pin one end of elastic to the garment and pin the other end with a large safety pin. Thread elastic through casing; sew ends together.

four of this shape will make either dress
or shirt above. the measurements need not
be exact as gathering with elastic or
drawstring creates proper fit.

the dress   step 1 - join side seams of body
·········   step 2 - sew sleeve seams
             step 3 - join sleeve to body
             step 4 - sew ribbon inside neck
                       to hold elastic
             step 5 - sew ribbon under bustline
                       to hold elastic
             step 6 - hem cuffs for elastic

the shirt as above - skip step 5.
·········

Mexican peasant blouse

Cut out these rectangles: (2 each)

A: ½ bust measurement plus 3 inches.

B: above chest to hemline

C: ½ chest (above bust) measurement

D: distance around arm socket plus 3 inches

E: 3 inches

F: distance over shoulder from the place where chest measurement was

G: sleeve length

H: neck to shoulder point

1. sew shoulders to yoke:

2. gather body to yoke:

3. sew sides up to ½ D plus E:

4. join gussets to sleeves:

5. join sleeves to body:

6. embroider edges, yoke, & sleeves with blanket stitch and decorate.

67

embroidery.

keep embroidery thread neat by cutting into length you use and braiding together 3 colors. The threads come out one at a time.

blanket stitch:

1. make a knot by taking a stitch and going back through it (like a finishing knot. Knotting the thread before you stitch makes a lump. This goes for all hand sewing).

2. come up

3. take a stitch up and go under and up to the right

4. catch the first stitch

5. repeat 3 & 4

making a chain

beautiful for hems, borders, appliqué, pockets,

flower:

1.

2.

3.

4.

5.

6.

63

this smock-shirt is easy
to make & can be easily changed
to be a dress, baby's gown, etc.
the only part you measure is the yoke:

neck plus 1½"

width of back plus 1½" for seams

BACK

neck to shoulder

FRONT

width of chest plus 2½"

the front and back are the same ⟶

longer than width because you gather it.

arm hole

cut out a great big sleeve

length of arm plus a few inches ⟶

wrist

shoulder

it doesn't matter how big the front, back and sleeve are because
you gather them before sewing them on.

1. sew together the shoulder seams.

use a stitch that goes backward + forward
it's easier and stronger (see hand sewing)
your thread— the needle won't come if you double
un-threaded.

always make seams on the inside of
the shirt!

2. gather front + back and sew them to yoke.
leave ½"inch around neck folded out.

3. sew together sides until it looks
like a comfortable size sleeve-hole
is left at the tops of each side.

4. sew sleeves together ⟶

5. gather sleeves around
shoulder end and sew to
shirt. make most of the
gathers above yoke- bodice
seam—mainly on the back ⟶
of the shirt

6. hem the bottom and the wrists.
put elastic in the wrist hems.
trim the neck with braid or
seam binding.

rug samples
make a rug
fur scraps for
a winter blanket
seat covers & purses
from leather scraps

Patchwork Quilts

Old clothes, upholstery samples, sewing scraps, old
neckties — free beautiful material is everywhere.
The pattern above is made of identical pieces, as is
the one lower left. The lower right is identically
wide strips of various lengths (work from center).
When the patchwork is done, place it over a layer
of dacron batting or some layers of flannel and
back it with cloth. Either tie knots through the
layers every 6 inches or sew the layers together
making a pattern as you go (quilt). Bind the edges.

More Patchwork: Transparent drapes
of scarves, patchwork skirts,
appliqué pictures in patch designs.

71

remaking second-hand clothes

if blue jeans are too short, add a cuff at the bottom cut from one other pair of old jeans. To make bell-bottoms, split the outer seams and add triangles of cloth.

to "un-straight" an ivy league shirt, cut off the sleeves & add: one half of a skirt on each side. gather the hem at the shoulder and use waist band at wrist. the left-over sleeves become baby's pants.

a sport jacket with the sleeves cut off and a few alterations makes a vest.

a circular skirt, especially a quilted one, makes a warm cape or lining for a cape.

a lady's narrow skirt easily becomes the bodice of a blouse.

2 men's socks and a cardigan sweater make a baby's jump suit:

doilies & napkins have many uses. a washcloth makes a bib for baby.   72

in hues of the forest....

the colors of the woods are ever changing.
collect bark, leaves, twigs, berries, tea leaves,
coffee grounds; dye cloth & weaving yarns to
their shades. First boil your wool, silk, cotton,
flax (manmade fibers are difficult to dye) in
water (one gallon per pound) with alum (one or two
ounces per pound). This will make the dyes set in
permantently (alum is mordant). Then boil
the vegetable matter several hours, strain.
Then dip in the wool yarn or cloth, stir it.
Different soaking times bring different shades; also
different boiling times change the intensity, so
you may get several shades of the same color.

73

tie-dye is not difficult. Prepare the cloth
with alum & prepare the tint. Let the cloth dry.
Then bind it with string or rubber bands
in various places. Dip the tightly tied cloth
in dye — let it sit a few minutes in the dye.
Then let it dry. When dry, untie it, and
tie new places. You may dip only small
places, like the ends of little sections, to
give variation to the design. When completed
& dry, iron out the wrinkles.

74

inkle loom

4 inches between each set of pegs

these 3 distances should be equal

heddle up

A
B

bobbin with yarn

to thread: secure one
end to end peg and
wind yarn around
pegs as shown:
Every other time
go over peg A
instead of under B.
The ones that go
over A are heddled
with circles of yarn.
For unique patterns
heddle (& wind over
A) 2 strings in a row.
to change color tie a
new piece of yarn to
the original at the
starting point. When
all strings on the pegs,
are wound, weave the end
of the last over to the first,
untie it from peg, & tie them.

to weave: tie bobbin to one string
and push between upper & lower
strings. lower heddle by pulling
downward so lower strings
are above. Pass bobbin through.
Then raise heddles & repeat.

← heddles

frame loom
(for square pieces of cloth)

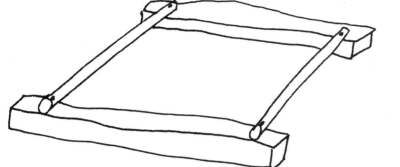

2 dowel sticks
(round) nailed
to 2 pieces of wood.

to thread: tie yarn (or thread) to one dowel. bring it over around under and back from the other. Then over and around the first, and so on, making a sort of figure 8 between the 2 dowels until it is all filled in.

to heddle: take another dowel of equal length and tie a string to one end of it. place it across loom and wind thread around the dowel, picking up one of the lower threads each time around. Place a strip of card board between threads (see below).

to weave: the first 2 or 3 inches use strips of rags to weave with since the threads are far apart. Side view:

heddle down (card flat)
• = where bobbin goes through
heddle up
(card up to facilitate bobbin passage)

already woven↗

the weaver's knot:

1. right (white) under left (black)

2. left up, around & over.

3. left tucks in under right

4. pull right

advantages:
all knots are on one side of fabric. since left thread is connected to work, to pull it would mar the work.

carving & leather tools:

a nail can be modified into a simple tool by changing it with a file

flatten the end to make a leather punch:

file an edge for carving:

file edge to a narrow width for delicate carving:

leather

remove all flesh and fat from hide and soak in brine a few days. Place on a smooth surface and scrape off all hair & grain. For hard leather - for shoes - leave hide to smoke. It must be away from heat but in the fumes. If you can secure the hide, hair side down, to a rock or tree, the birds will help scrape off the flesh.

For soft leather - simmer together equal parts animal brains and fat. Rub on to wet hide and leave 2 days. Wash hide clean and wring dry on poles going opposite ways (above). You can use tanbark oak (see fur) instead of animal brains & fat.

leather lacings

place knife blade in a wood surface, blade away from you, and put a nail ¼ inch away. Cut around the perimeter of the leather by pulling the strips toward you.

fur

remove flesh and fat, soak in brine. boil bark of tanbark oaktree (reddest of redwood trees - not an oak at all) until water turns red. add a handful of alum to set in hair. Soak hide in it all day. In the evening, stretch as above. When dry, work fat into hairless side of hide.

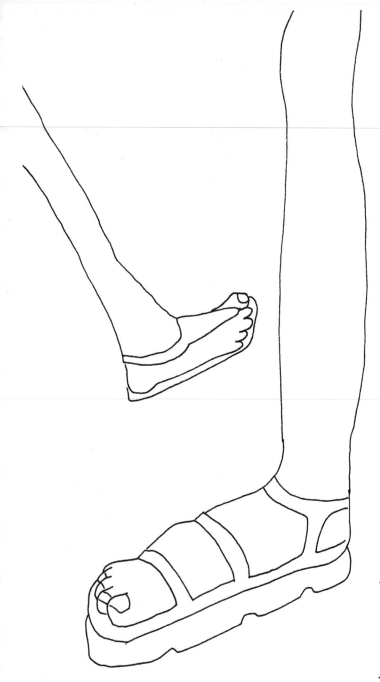

Sandals
° ° ° ° ° ° ° °

trace soles of feet on to paper. leave ¼ inch border for tire tread sandals, less for leather soles. cut with a crook neck knife

the tire treads and the soles of strong hard cowhide (identical size). For leather soles just cut 2 sets of identical soles. mark and cut holes in upper sole ½ inch away from foot where the straps go. Put straps through holes and glue together soles with barge's rubber cement.

use a beveler to smooth the edges of the straps. they will be stronger and cause fewer blisters (if any). You can get buckles from old shoes & belts at thrift stores and the local dump.

uppers – trace your foot. then draw line A (2 inches long) from your heel. line B is the distance across the highest part of your foot. uppers also have one inch border. punch holes on the sides for laces.

tongue

soles – trace your foot and leave one inch border.

moccasins

1. join the heel by overlapping one inch the ends of the uppers ......
2. overlap borders soles over uppers ......

3. you might have to punch the leather with a hammer and nail (or an awl) before you sew. a curved rug needle works well.
4. sew tongue to instep. the tongue is optional.
5. turn down the sides. you can cut fringe.
6. lacings weave through holes punched on sides and tie under tongue.
7. for eskimo boots add piece as shown (left).

distance around opening in shoe

80

whittling & wood carving

for decorative objects, soft wood without heavy grain
(white pine: ponderosa, california sugar pine, wisconsin
& michigan, also redwood, red cedar).

for functional objects, use hardwood (maple, bay,
oak, madrone, black walnut-).

It saves time & effort if you select a piece of wood close
to the size & shape of object you want to make. If
you can, cut out a rough outline with a band or
coping saw from larger pieces of wood.

Knife: a dull knife is much more likely to slip & cut you
than a sharp one. a dull knife, for woods purposes,
is non-functional. Carving tools are fun for
details but not necessary.

carving: cut with the grain of the wood as much
as possible. all long narrow pieces should
follow the grain of the wood.

sanding: always follow the grain of the wood except on
the end grain where it must cross.

pipe stem: hollow out with a red hot nail or bailing wire.

pipes: aim for bottom of bowl with hot nail. carve mouth piece; harden by holding over a candle flame.

Sanding: Use sharkskin or sandpaper (no. 1½ for coarse grained, no. 1 for light grained and no. ½ or no. 00 for very fine grain.

Finishing: To raise the grain, lightly sponge with water. If the wood gets fuzzy, resand with no. 0 or no. 00 paper. Then sand with no. 3/0 when dry. Then apply a water stain (a powdered water-soluble pigment) and wipe off excess with a cloth. let dry 12 hours. Then apply one coat of white shellac and one coat of varnish, let dry. Sand with 5/0 or 8/0 garnet paper, dust it off and apply one more coat of varnish and let it dry. Rub in pumice stone & crude oil.
Another finish is linseed (raw) oil. apply several coats 24 hours apart. Then melt beeswax in turpentine until the mixture is thick and apply many thin coats across the grain (allow each coat to dry before adding another) and rubbing with a soft cloth or chamois.

Polish: Raw nuts rubbed on wood give an oily polish.

clay occurs in the soil in many places and is easy to recognize: it is fine & dusty or hard during the summer and a fine mud in winter. When you dig it out it will have sand, stones, & organic decay mixed in. To purify: mix clay with water in a large bowl. When it is dissolved the impurities will settle to the bottom. Scoop clay off top. Repeat several times until pure. Mix new clay with an old batch and/or store it indoors a few months. Ageing improves the quality of the clay. Mixing in grog (powder of fired clay from ground-up broken pots) insures uniform drying, minimum shrinkage, and reduces the tendency to slump when molded.

Clay makes wonderful free-form objects, decorative and *functional* (spoons, beads, bowls, candleholders, ad infinitum)

there are many ways to make a pot. One is the coil method. roll out 1" coils of clay and form the pot thus:

bottom

sides

smooth surfaces with a soup of clay & water:

another method is throwing on a wheel. a japanese potter's wheel is the simplest kind.

Bake ceramic pieces by leaving them near your fire a few weeks or build a kiln...
(next page)

another method is to line a container with cheesecloth, roll out clay 1 inch thick, and line the container with clay. When firm, remove clay from mold.

to build a kiln: clear
a wide area of all brush
arrange a floor of porous
insulating fire bricks (see
appendix A). Stack pots on top
and stack the light porous
bricks around and over them.
Build a big hot fire around
the kiln and keep it going
at least six hours for the
bisque (first) firing. (a good
project for a cold night). Then
let the whole thing cool 24
hours, and unstack it. For the
second firing, (when you apply
a glaze), place a little ceramic cone
(from art supply store) behind one removable
brick. When it has melted, the
glaze should be done; let the fire
die down. For these glazes use cones
size 012 to 08:
    transparent glaze
        gerstley borate 80 parts
        nepheline syanite 20 parts
    pearly grey glaze
        gerstley borate 50
        borax (20 mule team) 50
    for red, add to the pearly grey:
        copper 10 parts
        rutile 10 parts

waxy matte glaze
    gerstley borate 30 parts
    kaolin 20 parts
    silica (flint) 10 parts
waxy off-white glaze
    gerstley borate 80 parts
    talc 20 parts
blue: add 10 parts cobalt to any glaze
green: add 10 parts potassium dichromate
ground up glass bottles can also be
added – milk of magnesia blue,
root beer brown, wine bottle green,
broken windowpane white etc.

You can also decorate with slip
(water with clay mixed in to a
soupy consistency), which could
be red, yellow or white, depending
on the clay used, and do a matte
or transparent glaze over it. For
a rough texture on the outside
of a bowl, add sand or grog to the
slip. To apply glaze: mix the
components with water to the
consistency of slip. Daub on with
a soft brush. apply 4 generous
coats. Let it dry thoroughly.
Stack as before and fire until
cones melt. For food dishes the
glaze must be smooth and
inert. glazes containing lead
can cause a cumulative poisoning
if used to serve acid foods or
to cook in. (all above are non-leaded).

community candles: melt wax in
an oil drum. Prepare a hoop
smaller than the circumference of
the drum. Hang wicks from it.
Attach the hoop to an overhead pulley.
So you can raise and lower the
hoop each time you want to dip. Cut
off the ends when they get too big.
To harden wax: add 2 ounces alum per pound of
wax during melting.
To prepare wicks: tightly braided string, dipped in vinegar
and dried thoroughly, works well. Candles
burn brighter if you braid in some wire.
Fancy: dip fresh flowers in clear wax and attach to
wet candles. Braid several pliable candles.

87

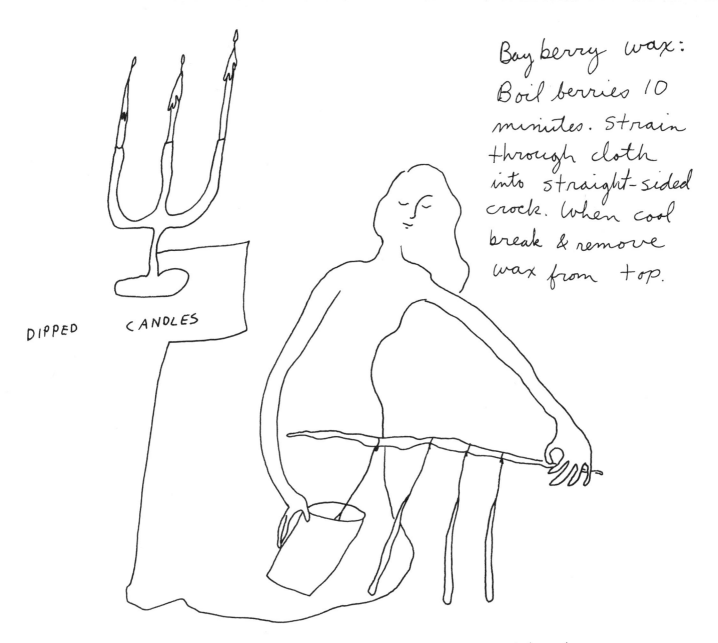

DIPPED CANDLES

Bayberry wax:
Boil berries 10
minutes. Strain
through cloth
into straight-sided
crock. When cool
break & remove
wax from top.

melt wax in a coffee can. color it by
melting in crayons. Tie pieces of string
on a branch and dip one by one until
candle looks thick enough. the candles
can bend around while dipping — they dry
hard — so it doesn't matter if the wax container
isn't as tall as the candles.
the cheapest wax is used candle butts from
thrift stores. Use the heaviest string available.

88

to begin – melt some wax in a can over a high flame. for separate colors use several cans and color with wax crayons. Keep wax liquid over a low flame. Scent with incense oils.

floating candle: pour wax on a flat surface. Form petals by pressing against a small candle which is the center of floating candle. continue making petals until you have three or four rows.

sand candle: form mold by digging into wet sand. Tie wick to a piece of coat hanger wire and bury wire at bottom of mold. hold wick up with one hand and pour in wax.

carved candle: an old milk carton or paper cup with hole in bottom to drive through wick is the mold. Seal hole with wax before pouring in the alternate layers of colored wax (allow each layer to dry before adding new one). Tear off mold when dry and carve with a knife. Finish edges of carving by smoothing with a lighted match.

agate candle: mold is made from aluminum foil in a strange shape. Make hole in bottom for wick – seal with wax. Pour in alternate layers of colored wax.

ice candle: mold is a paper cup or milk carton. add wick as above. Fill with ice cubes and pour in hot wax. Ice melts and leaves cubic holes in candle. this candle burns fast but makes interesting shapes.

canned candle: Remove ends from a tin can and pierce sides decoratively. place inside candle mold which is about an inch larger in diameter. Fill with wax. as candle burns, the can appears and casts interesting shadows. a lacey pierced can (make lines with acetylene torch) makes a lantern for any candle).

EXOTIC CANDLES

eucalyptus pods and cloves and whole allspice can be soaked overnight and pierced with a needle making very fragrant necklaces. Pierce the cloves through the stem.

limpet shells , sections of bamboo, whittled knobs of wood (pierce with a hot nail), stones or marbles bound with thread (see below),

and papier maché (soak shredded newspaper in flour & water and form into balls around nails. When dry, remove nail) make beautiful beads.

bound marble: place beads as shown. lace thread through outer beads for "longitudes". thread a needle and spiral back for "latitudes"

melon, pumpkin & squash seeds must be washed, then soaked overnight. While wet they can be pierced with a needle and strung on nylon fishing line or heavy waxed thread.

beads

clay beads are simple to make. (form little balls & pierce with a nail. smooth with water, dry, & fire). Instead of glazing them, one can mosaic them with tiny smooth pebbles from the seashore (use epoxy glue). 90

Art Supplies

quills for writing. cut off tops and tie in loose bundles. Place upright in 1 quart boiling water with 2 tablespoons of alum. Boil 'til clear and dry in the sun (for stiffer more brittle quills, use more alum).

paint brush the indians of the high desert prepared brushes for painting pottery by chewing the wide end of the yucca spike until maleable and spreading the fibers.

charcoal for drawing. willow makes the best charcoal for this purpose. Gently shape it with a knife into crayon sizes and simmer them in melted wax for 30 minutes. Let them dry on a paper towel. After drawing with these charcoals, warm the back side of the drawing and the lines will become permanent.

tracing paper saturate ordinary writing paper with gasoline with a brush, wipe it off and let it dry.

Sandpaper. stretch out a piece of very heavy paper and cover it with glue. Sift onto it powdered pumice stone.

91

sponge brush. (for poster paint or water color) makes a soft impressionist painting or a geometric design. Just cut a hole in a small piece of sponge & add a stick as a handle (glue in with epoxy). Dip in paint and gently pat on paper. If you don't have epoxy, a rubber band might work.

window flowers. fold up a paper towel in quarters and then into triangular eighths like you would to cut out a snowflake. Drop spots of food coloring on the towel. Then unfold it. The colors are brilliant and the translucent towel looks pretty with sun shining through it

Splatter prints. dip an old tooth brush in poster paint and rub in over a piece of screen. The paint sprays onto the page below. When you put something, like a leaf for example, on the page you get a white space in a leaf shape. Try different colors & things together.

large & small baskets:
a simple baby's bed
which may even be suspended
from the ceiling (above).
made by crossing
8 long thin poles and
lashing thinner
greenwood sticks in
circles, creating an
inverted dome shape.
a pillow in the center
makes a mattress.

baskets can be made of
whatever grows around
you. Soak your materials
overnight to insure
pliability. Cross the heavier
strips in the center and
weave with the lighter
material spiralling out-
ward. Willow and reeds are
tradional. Hemp fiber is a
useful by-product for baskets.

packing frame is of lashed hardwood sticks. The outer stick should be soaked over night so it will bend into an oval. The baby carrier is the same 2 belt device shown on the hanging swing with a spring (bounces). The bouncing board (below) is four huge springs attached to two big square boards. Fun to jump on. Boards & boxes & big pieces of cloth are good toys; you can build your own little house

Toys You Can Make

stuffed dolls &

bean bags . . . . .

1. Trace shape onto cloth (2 thicknesses with the right side together)

2. Draw a margin around each shape (no shape should be less than 1" wide, otherwise it is hard to turn them right side out).

3. Cut out around margin lines.

4. Sew together around lines of original shape. Leave 2 inches or more unsewn so you can turn it right side out. Use a pencil to force ends of arms & legs rightside out.

5. Stuff dolls & soft animals with either nylon foam rubber scraps (from sponge factories or sometimes sold as pillow stuffing) or old nylon stockings. Both launder well. Sew up opening.

6. Stuff bean bags with beans, sand, grains (millet works well), dried used tea leaves etc. Sew up opening.

7. Add eyes, hair, clothes etc.

More Toys You Can Make

an abacus (counting device) is easy to make: drill holes in 3 sticks of wood (space your holes evenly) and insert wires through holes. each heavy wire (coathanger or even metal rods or thin wood dowels) should have several beads on it to count with.

Children can make:

floating toy: take a long, lightweight piece of cloth and place a few beans or some sand at one end and tie it with string. Throw it in the air and it will come down with the long tail of cloth floating behind it.

animal toys: stick toothpicks into peanuts (in shells)

stuffed toys: are easily made by stuffing socks with scraps of cloth, binding them shut and decorating:

3 socks   1 sock

bamboo rattles:
bind two pieces
of well-seasoned
bamboo 4 inches
from the top.
Slit bamboo every
½ inch all the way
around down to
the binding.

lip
line

flutes: cut dry oat straws
so that a solid
section remains
at top (see picture).
Slit from just
below section.
insert flute
in mouth up
to lip line and
blow hard.
you can
burn in
finger holes
with a
hot pin.

anklets &
wristlets for
dancers:
sew little
bells onto
leather or
heavy cloth
strips. Shake
wrists to
rhythm.

oboe: hollow out a long root
from a bamboo plant with a
hot metal rod. burn in finger
holes. Make a reed of an oat
straw (see flutes) and insert at top.

rasping
gourd:
hollow out &
dry a long
gourd. With
a hot wire,
burn in
some
transverse
grooves (or
carve them
in).

water drum: a vessel
of metal with a ½ inch
of water in the bottom.
Turn it with one hand
while tapping with the
other.

claves: dry
and age two
large pieces
of bamboo,
cut equal
length.

maracas:
hollow out and
dry gourds in
sun. Place
pebbles or beans
inside. Add smooth
sticks through center
sealing holes.

a funky tin slide guitar
(played with a "bottleneck")

use steel strings & tuning pegs from a guitar.
construct a rectangular frame of steel
bars. it must be strong or the steel strings will
make it buckle

add wooden ends and a tuning end:

cover with tin. a gasoline can works fine:

(top view)

(copy frets off a guitar)

the bridges are spikes with grooves. action is so
high the strings never touch the guitar:

pentatonic tuning
for autoharp

several strings in
a row may all be
the same note.

GDG A B D E G A B

G major tuning:
G - B - D G - B - D
G minor tuning:
G - B♭ - D - G - B♭ - D

these make a music
reminiscent of Italian
Renaissance songs.

tunings for the guitar

In addition to classical
tuning (E - A - D - G - B - E),
there are numerous
tunings which adapt
well to ragas and
other music out of
the western structures.

D - modal tuning:
D - A - D - G - B - D
D - open tuning:
D - A - D - A - D - D
D - minor tuning:
D - A - D - F - A - D

D - major tuning:
D - A - D - F# - A - D
D 7th tuning:
D - A - D - F# - C - D

zither
an autoharp with the
"machines" removed
may be tuned open.
It can be played with
sticks or feathers or
plucked & strummed
with the fingers.

100

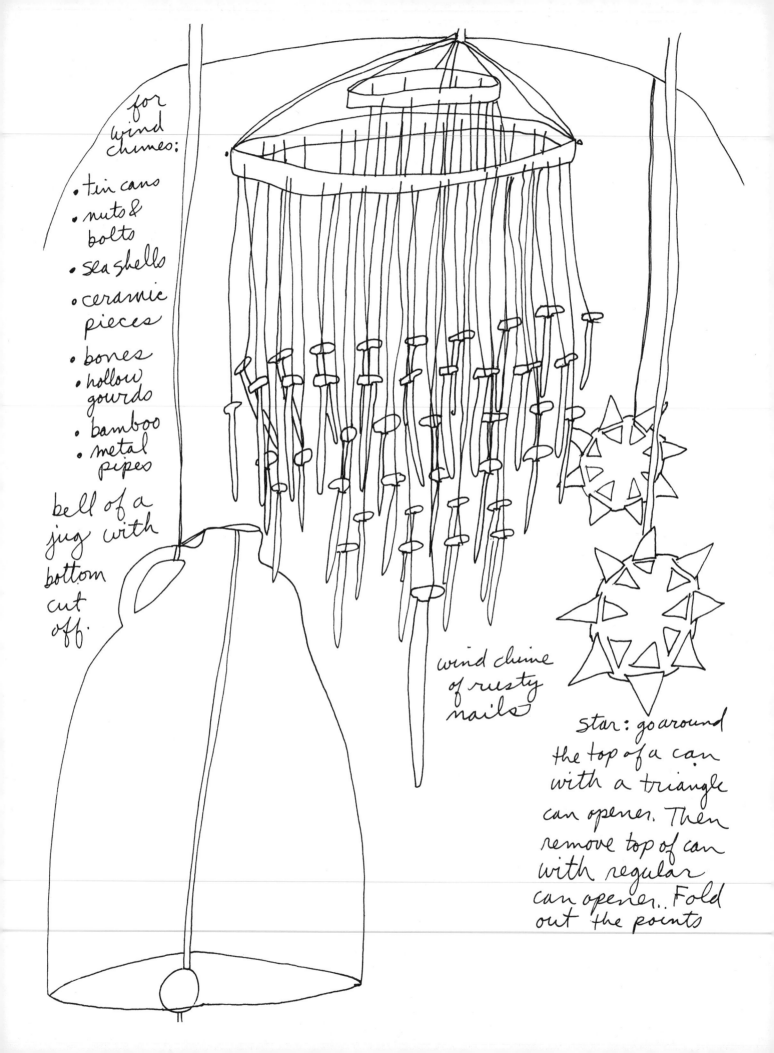

for
wind
chimes:

- tin cans
- nuts & bolts
- sea shells
- ceramic pieces
- bones
- hollow gourds
- bamboo
- metal pipes

bell of a jug with bottom cut off.

wind chime of rusty nails

Star: go around the top of a can with a triangle can opener. Then remove top of can with regular can opener. Fold out the points

besides being invaluable in jug bands, glass jugs make dandy bells. They are great as individual green houses for struggling young plants. and they are used for carrying water to campsites where it is not readily available. Plastic containers are lighter for water.

how to cut the bottoms off glass jugs:
cut around the bottom with a glass cutter.
Dip the jug in hot water, then in ice water.

bells — hang a wooden bead from the handle as a bell clapper

green house — place it right over the plant.

jug for band — stretch some inner-tube over the open end and secure with a leather thong.
Vary the pitch of the jug by pressing and releasing the rubber.

A BAMBOO FLUTE

bamboo should be completely dried out - yellow not green. drive a metal shaft heated to red hot through sections in bamboo so that you have one long tube closed at one end.

Place mouth hole 1/7 to 1/8 the length of flute from the closed end. Burn through with a hot metal rod or welding tip on a torch. mouth hole should be oval (longer in the direction of flute length). burn in finger holes where they are comfortable.

the chinese were once very hip to living in nature. the Tao Te Ching of Lao-Tzu says:
"the highest motive is to be like water. Water is essential to all living things, yet it demands no pay or recognition. Rather it flows humbly to the lowest level.
Nothing is weaker than water; yet for overcoming what is hard and strong, nothing surpasses it."

the I Ching (the book of changes) restates the philosophy of the Tao in sixty-four poems. ask the I Ching a question by throwing coins or counting yarrow sticks. the answer is always worthy of meditation

hatha yoga keeps
you stoned.

asana (posture)
tones the body and
makes it healthy
and beautiful.

Pranayama
(breathing exercises)
quiets the mind;
thinking and
breathing proceed
at the same rate.

These are but two
of the eight steps
of raja yoga.
They lead to
meditation and
enlightenment.

the best book
I have ever
seen on hatha
yoga is Light
on Yoga by
B. K. S. Iyengar.

mantra
is a simple
meditation.
Repeat over &
over a phrase
to change your
consciousness.

"A-U-M"

"Om mané padmé hum"

"Haré krishna haré krishna
krishna krishna haré haré
haré rama haré rama
rama rama haré haré"

"Shanti" (peace)

"Nam Myo Ho Renge Kyo"

fasting cleanses:
before & after a
fast eat only
laxative foods
(dried fruit). During
a fast, drink fruit
juice. Be prepared:
your body will go
through many changes.

106

how to slow down...

find a little bit of land somewhere and
plant a carrot seed. Now sit down and
watch it grow. When it is fully grown
pull it up and eat it.

— Stephen Gaskin

gardening.

the department of agriculture and the rodale books on organic farming can supply you with bountiful information on gardening. (see useful books). Just to give an idea of what is involved, here are the major tasks of the season:

1. planning: irrigation: for a few rows without hassle, plant on a bank of a stream. otherwise, plan your rows according to accessability of water on downhill irrigation ditches.
   difficulty of growing versus desirability of crop: tomatoes & potatoes are not easy to grow, but potatoes are cheap to buy and don't change in storage, whereas a vine-ripened tomato is worth the work. consider your climate, soil, local pests, and personal taste in vegetables. Some crops are desirable simply for their outstanding nutritional value (soybeans, kale, sunflowerseeds, parsley, alfalfa, rosa rugosa -for rose hips-, collards, mustard & turnip greens, garlic). luffa gourds can be grown & used as sponges.

if you have beehives—alfalfa, buckwheat, orange trees and sunflowers may be considered as honey plants, too. Bees will pollinate your crops.

planting guide . . . . . .

crop	amount of seed per 100 row-feet	yield per 100 row feet
bush beans	1 pound	50 pounds
beets	2 ounces	100 pounds
broccoli	50 plants	50 pounds
cabbage	50 plants	100 pounds
carrots	1 ounce	100 pounds
cauliflower	45 plants	45 heads
corn	4 ounces	100 ears
cucumbers	½ ounce	150 pounds
egg plant	50 plants	125 fruit
lettuce	½ ounce	50 pounds
melons	½ ounce	50 fruit
onions	300 plants or 1 ounce seed	85 pounds
parsley	¼ ounce	50 pounds
peas	1 pound	40 pounds
radishes	1 ounce	1200 fruit
soybeans	½ pound	50 pounds
squash	½ ounce	100 fruit
tomatoes	25-50 plants	200 pounds
turnips	½ ounce	100 pounds

Choose bug-resistant varieties and introduce the natural enemies of your local pests to the area rather than resort to poisonous sprays.

2. equipment: hoe, shovel, rake, spade. for a one acre plot, a 3 to 5 horsepower rotar-tiller (runs on gasoline), and optionally a compost shredder. Stakes, wire, wire cutters. Fencing. a wheelbarrow, a hose or watering can. Bushel baskets for harvesting. Flats, peat pots and greenhouse. a storage cellar for root crops, squashes and apples in winter, vegetables and fruits of all kinds in summer (very handy if it has a door directly to outdoors) large kitchen with equipment for canning, drying, grinding. a hand press for apple juice if you have apple trees. gardening books & of course, seeds.

3. Starting seeds: Some plants, like tomatoes, eggplant & broccoli are best started indoors in peatmoss cups or egg shells. The whole container goes into the earth with the young plant.

4. preparing the soil: first clear away rocks and bushes. Then plow with rotar-tiller (or with oxen & hand-plow,) then hoe it to break up the clods into fine earth. then add compost, manure, granite dust, etc and stir it under. allow it to sit a week or more before planting if possible so the fertilizer won't burn the seedlings. prepare mounds for the melons, squashes, cucumbers: dig holes one foot in diameter, one foot deep. add a shovel-full of compost. cover each hole with a mound of fine earth one foot high and make a little moat around it (when vines get 6 inches high, water them only in the moat - the roots will grow deeper.)

5. Planting: follow directions on seed packets. If you plant each crop over a series of weeks, you will have a continuous supply.

6. compost: build a sandbox-like structure two feet high and cover it with a heavy black plastic sheet (to accelerate rotting and to keep flies from breeding in it— keep it covered at all times!) Place in it all organic waste * (keep a bucket in the kitchen to collect it) (* except meat scraps, which attract skunks.) manure, leaf mold (rotting leaves from forest floor) and mineral supplements like granite dust (find out what your soil lacks). chopped sea vegetation is rich in minerals. Stir well, shred by machine if possible. age 6 months before using. Note: non-organic wastes like metal & glass can be crushed and buried in a trench surrounding the garden fence. This keeps out gophers & rabbits. All other wastes—wood, cloth, etc, can be burned in a deep pit and the ashes buried or used as snail fencing: paint boards with motor oil and cover with ashes. fence your vegetable beds with these; snails won't go over them. a dish of beer left on the ground is also lethal to snails.

7. thinning: When young plants get 6 inches high, thin out the smaller ones according to directions on the seed packets.

8. mulch: a layer of sawdust, straw, leaf mold or wood chips protects the soil around the plant from drying out, conserves water, enriches the soil. apply one inch thick to within ½ inch of stems.

9. Stakes: vines—like peas, tomatoes & beans need stakes or else little fences to grow around. Helps support plant when in fruit.

10. daily care: keep plants free of weeds (mulch helps that too), and water according to directions for individual crop (in books). It's best to water just after sundown. Fertilize with "manure tea": dissolve well-rotted manure in water and use to water plants — only use a small amount. All plants, animals & people respond to love. Sing to your garden. Young plants flourish under the protection of individual green-houses made by removing the bottoms of glass jugs & placing over plants (see "jugs").

11. harvesting: by taking the outer leaves of the lettuce, cabbage, etc, you get a continuous supply, without killing plant; the same plant may live several seasons, producing more each year. 114

earthworms turn decay & waste into rich odorless humus earth. They are the best compost shredders going. To greatly enrich your garden's topsoil, set up a worm colony in your compost box. Keep it

a gardener's allies

moist & shady. Start with sifted dirt & well rotted organic compost and you will gradually get to where you can give them fresh organic garbage & they will take care of it. See the earth worms turn garbage into treasure.

lady bugs, praying mantids, & birds protect your garden from assault by insects.

horses have a lot to contribute to your garden. Just offer to clean someone's stable and take a truckload home to your garden.

chickens require almost no care at all. They will nest in a cardboard box or in a bush. They don't need fences. Feed them table scraps and maybe a little grain feed. You may add apple cider vinegar to their water

keep layering straw over the chicken shit & feathers in their yard & house. at the end of the season you will have some good compost.

for egg production, feed them 16% egg laying mash.

the eggs you buy in supermarkets come from hens that live in shaded cages and are fed methedrine so they lay more & eat less. your eggs will come from happy fertile hens who dance freely in the sun. like you.

fruit trees

you can have a succession of fruits ripening from early spring to midwinter if you plant a variety of trees. Plant berry bushes, too. Find out which grow in your climate. Write to the dept. of agriculture or read the organic gardening books (j.i. rodale) for information on care of trees. Besides fruit, there's nuts, carob pods, avocados, olives. Dwarf fruit trees bear earlier and are easier to harvest than standard trees.

canning

Step 1: choose sound, slightly under-ripe fruits and vegetables. For pickles or preserves see their respective pages. Wash, cut, peel and pit as necessary. Soups, juices and aspics prepare as usual. Prepare vegetables by cooking until just underdone. Use cooking water to can.

Step 2: Scald jars by pouring boiling water over them and leaving them in boiled water until you are ready to use them. Boil lids.

Step 3: Pack raw fruit or prepared foods into jars. Pack no higher than one half inch from top. Pack corn or lima beans, beans & peas no higher than one inch from top.

Step 4: Pour in water, brine, vinegar or syrup within 1½ inches of top. Syrup for fruit: heat together 2 cups honey and 3¾ cups water. Whole cloves, cinnamon, etc. may be added to fruit. Wipe jars clean, place on scalded lids, screw bands on tight. Pickles & preserves need no processing.

step 5: jellies & jams may be sealed with paraffin. Pour simmering jam into scalded jars and allow to cool. Remove all particles of jelly from jar above jelly. Melt paraffin and pour on a thin layer. Rotate the glass so paraffin coats sides above jelly. Pour off excess paraffin, place scalded lid on glass, label and store.

step 6: Place jars on rack and lower into boiling water of canning cauldron. Leave in fruits 25 minutes. Juices require 10 minutes; soup stock requires 180 minutes; all green vegetables, onions, squash, pumpkin require 3 hours; tomatoes take 35 minutes; root vegetables like carrots & turnips take 2 hours, peppers, 2 hours; cabbage 2 hours; cauliflower and broccoli 1½ hours. Remove and set jars uptight in several thicknesses of cloth to cool gradually. Jars might crack if left in a cool place. When jars are cold, test for seal by tapping lid with a spoon. It should ring, not make a dull tap. Press down lid. If it can be moved at all, open and re-can the contents. Remove the screw bands, label the jars and store in a cool dry place. Vegetables, especially beans, if imperfectly canned, can cause botulism.

into a clean jar put
cut-up garlic and dill
weed. then some
slightly under-ripe
(hard) vegetables:
Pickling cucumbers
green tomatoes
lemon cucumbers
onion slices
hot peppers
pimiento
cauliflowerlets
carrots
olives
boil together water, salt
and apple cider vinegar.
The proportions can vary
according to taste.
pour liquid into jar
over vegetables & spices.
when it is cold it is
ready to eat, but sitting
a week first improves
it.

when preparing for future use,
boil jars before using and after
sealing them.

Ambrosia Sauce

make apple sauce, but use pears, peaches, whatever fresh fruit you have. add raisens & dried fruit, cook 'til tender, Flavor with honey, orange & lemon juice and grated peel, wine, grated coconut. Pour over fresh fruit salad or a cake.

ORANGE MARMALADE

Slice 4 oranges & 3 lemons. add 6 cups water. Leave overnight. Cook 30 minutes. Leave overnight again. add honey, less than equal parts. cook 10 minutes. Pour into sterile jars & seal with paraffin.

Rose Honey:

warm, don't boil, honey with crushed rose petals. Let stand 3 days. Strain.

Berry Preserves

wash, stem berries. Drain. Cook berries over low flame with a little water 'til juice is mostly extracted add equal amount of honey stirring constantly. careful: honey boils over easier than sugar. pour into sterile jars, seal with paraffin.

Chestnut jam

Shell, boil 'til tender, and chop fine several pounds of chestnuts. Simmer 'til thick with an equal amount of honey, and 3 teaspoons orange flower water and ¼ teaspoon vanilla per pound of nuts. pour into hot sterile glasses. Seal with paraffin.

Rose Petal Jam

a traditional gift to lovers in greece. gather several quarts rose petals. stack and cut off white tips. Chop fine. Simmer together 10 minutes honey (1 part) water (1 part) add petals (2 parts), 1 teaspoon lemon juice. Simmer 30 minutes and pour into sterilized jars.

APPLE SAUCE

core (peel if you wish) apples and place in pot over low flame with water ⅓ as full as the pot is full of apples. Stir. It will melt down in 15 or 20 minutes into apple sauce. add cinnamon or berries if you want. See canning instructions.

Apple butter

cook apple sauce in a heavy pot over a low flame (lid off) 3 or 4 hours until dark brown. Very Sweet.

Rose Hip Conserve

grind fresh rose hips coarsely and force through a strainer to remove seeds. Liquify in a blender with water. add equal or maybe ⅓ as much honey. Pour into sterilized jars, seal, and place jars in boiling water 15 minutes. Store in cool place. Heat cuts down vitamin C.

you can dry apples
pears, peaches, plums,
cherries figs, grapes,
coconut, guavas &
asparagus, beans,
beets, corn, cabbage
and 'others' (see below)

SUN-DRYING FRUITS
AND VEGETABLES

the entire process needs
cleanliness of hands &
equipment.

1. select sound ripe produce
(not bruised or over-ripe)
2. wash and peel, pit or slice
as needed. Slice big fruit thin.
3. steam the vegetables in a
basket over boiling water
(see chart for time)
4. place on trays one layer thick
and cover with a cloth or wire
mesh to keep off dirt & insects.
5. turn over produce two or three
times a day.
6. test for doneness by squeezing
produce in your hand. It should
leave no moisture and should
fall apart when you let go.
Berries should rattle in trays.
7. Place in a basket for a few days
and stir three times a day
8. Store in closed containers in
a cool dark place.
9. To restore vegetables, soak a few
hours before using.

onions, sunflowers, garlic, herbs,
peanuts, red peppers, and beans
must be dried before storing.
remove seeds from green chile peppers.

vegetable steaming chart		
prepared vegetable	steaming time	
asparagus tips	4-5 minutes	
green string beans	15-20 "	
beets (no tops)	30-45	then peel & slice
broccoli	8-10	
cabbage (shredded)	8-10	
carrots rutabagas & turnips	8-10	then slice
corn	10-15	then cut from cob
shelled peas	10	
shoestring cut potato	4-6	
spinach & greens	4	don't wad on drying trays
sweet potato, squash & pumpkin (peeled & sliced)	til tender	
tomatoes - dip in boiling water - then cold water - peel - cut up.		

apple cider vinegar

in a wide-mouthed
jar or crock place
apple peelings & cores.
cover with water and
add more fruit from
time to time. a foam
becomes apparent on
top. This is called
"mother of vinegar".
add some to sweet
cider and it will
turn to vinegar in
a few days (depends
on heat.) The water
from the crock is
also strong vinegar.

flavored vinegars

heat one quart
red wine vinegar
and pour into
a quart jar. add
one clove of garlic
a piece of chile
pepper and
several sprigs of
tarragon   or
1 quart washed
nasturtium
flowers   or

Several sprigs of
mint   or

3 ounces curry
powder.
Let stand 2 months,
Strain, bottle.

124

wine made of fruit

currant mead

dissolve 4½ pounds honey in 1 gallon water, boiling hot. Leave til cool, add 3 quarts red currant juice, 1 pound chopped raisins. Place in a stone crock. Make a paste of one cake (teaspoon) yeast* with water and spread on toast. Float the toast on the liquid. Cover and let stand in a warm place 16 days. Skim, strain thru nylon cloth, let stand 10 days, siphon into bottles, seal with corks. Wine varies in fermenting time. When the yeastly taste is gone it's ready. Other fruits, not citrus fruits though, can be used (cherries, peaches, pears, apricots etc.) *wine-maker's yeast

apple mead

mix equal parts raw honey and raw apple cider, stir until honey dissolves. Let stand in a covered stone crock in a warm place. Skim when it stops "working", siphon and strain through nylon cloth, bottle, seal, and age it, if you can.

125

wine made of flowers

Elder blow wine

wash & drain
6 cups elder
flowers. Place
them in a crock.
Cover with a syrup
of 10 pounds honey
and 3 gallons water.
(heat, then cool it down).
add 1 cake yeast to the
juice of 3 oranges & one
lemon. Combine with
flowers, syrup, & 2 pounds
raisins. Let stand 10 days.
Strain, let stand in a
covered crock 4 months.
Bottle. Store 6 months
in cellar before using.

dandelion wine

combine & let stand
in a covered crock
9 days: 4 quarts water
and 4 quarts dandelion
blossoms. Strain (squeeze)
flowers. To water extract
add 3 pounds honey
3 sliced lemons, one
cake yeast. Let stand
in crock 9 days. Then
strain it into a jug.
Leave it, cork off, until it
stops working; then
cork it up.

clover wine

boil together for 20 minutes:
2 quarts clover blossoms, 2 quarts water.
pour into a crock, let stand 24 hours.
Strain. To water add 2 pounds
honey, 1½ teaspoons dry yeast, one
sliced orange & one sliced lemon.
Proceed as above.

126

home grown

to start seeds before the
last frost: place rich soil
in a can or large paper
cup and water twice a
day. they should have
¼" soil above them and
a foot of soil below if they
are to have room to grow.
cover with plastic. an
indoor catbox works well.
a mantra, such as AUM,
recited over the seedlings
will enhance their growth;
they respond to love.
after the last frost: transplant
the young plants in a
sunny place with a piece
of clear plastic over them to
retain moisture until they
are hardy. Sow seeds
directly in warm moist
soil ¼" deep; pack soil down.
during growth: Cut back
plant when 3 feet high so it
will branch out and have
more flower heads. Cut down
the male plants. Water
plants daily.
harvest when the seeds turn
dark grey, hang plants upside
down in the shade one week.
Then sun-dry them thoroughly.
to cure sprinkle with equal parts
brandy & water. Dry in the sun.

elegant unbaked confections

moroccan surprise

classical: grind up:
1 teaspoon peppercorns,
1 whole nutmeg
4 5 sticks cinnamon
1 teaspoon coriander
1 or more lids (cleaned)
one handful each
dates, dried figs
almonds, peanuts.
combine & roll into balls.

whimsical: to above add
any of the following:

honey   sunflower or
coconut   sesame seed meal
carob powder   grated orange rind
toasted wheat germ   banana
Stoney-butter (recipe below)

Stoney butter grind seeds
& stems. Simmer gently
with butter 4 hours.
Strain. use butter in
any confection recipe.

fruit cake

chop pitted dried fruits. grind
together: nuts, roasted soybeans.
Combine with any or all: shredded
coconut, sesame or sunflower seeds (or
seed meal), toasted wheat germ, crumbs,
toasted grains, grated orange or lemon peel

mashed ripe banana, honey,
oil or tahini. Place in a
loaf pan. pour on fruit juice.
Place a weight on top. Chill
24 hrs. to 2 weeks. It
ferments. Turn out on a
platter & slice thin.

128

cow's milk separates into cream and milk in an hour.

Scoop the cream off and shake it in a glass jar a few hours. The butter lumps get bigger & bigger. When you have a big lump, salt it if you like, and store in a crock in a cool place.

fresh, cow's milk

cottage cheese . . . . heat sour milk to wrist temperature and strain through a diaper or cheesecloth. use the whey for baking. mix salt with the curds.

hard cheese . . . . heat one gallon milk (can be sour) to wrist temperature and add one crushed junket rennet tablet. When solid, salt it and drain in a cheesecloth. age a few days (longer is better). you can smoke it in a smoke house.

buttermilk . . . . add ½ cups buttermilk to 4 cups milk & let thicken at room temperature. store in a cool place.

sour cream . . . . add to 1 cup heavy cream: 1 teaspoon lemon juice or vinegar or 2 teaspoons sour milk. let stand 'til thick.

cream cheese . . . . let cream sour 2 days. drain through cheese cloth. Form curds into cakes. Chill.

heat milk to wrist temperature (don't boil)
and stir in one tablespoon yogurt per
pint of milk. Pour into small glass jars.
Leave them in the sun all day if it is
warm and sunny. Or leave in a warm
place (near stove). Or if it's sunny, but not
warm, leave jars in a black box in the sun all
day. Or put yogurt in a thermos bottle.
Instant milk can also be used — or even
evaporated milk — restored to normal consistency.

YOGURT...

Store in a cool place after it reaches desired tanginess.
Yogurt culture destroys toxic bacteria in the colon.

1½ cups dried beans or peas serves 6.

Split peas, lentils, pinto beans & black eye peas can be cooked without pre-soaking. All others should be soaked all day or overnight. Keep them cold so they don't ferment.

½ cup dried grains serves 1. Cook over a high flame 'til boiling, then reduce heat and cook 'til all water is absorbed. 1 part grain to 2 parts water for all whole grains except millet,

grain casserole
mix together:
cooked grains or beans
chopped nuts
raw or cooked vegetables
sprouts
herbs, soy sauce
one raw egg
place in a large greased baking dish, top with grated cheese bake 20 minutes.

beans

grains

cereals

cook beans in the water you soaked them in, simmer 2 or 2½ hours. Soybeans may take even longer. Cumin seed, onion, garlic, bacon (raw), salt or soy sauce may be added while cooking.

which needs 4 parts water, and cornmeal which is 1 to 3. Buckwheat groats should be roasted in oil first, then a mixture of egg, salt, and 1½ parts water poured over. Cook until water is absorbed.

"macroburgers"
in a blender mix to a paste:
2 cups cooked soy beans
2 tablespoons soy sauce
sage & oregano
stir in:
1 cup dry roasted rolled oats
1 cup cooked millet
chopped onions, garlic and other raw or cooked vegetables.
Fry as patties in oil.

MUESLI

ROAST: Rolled oats
wheat flakes, rye
flakes add
soy grits
sesame seeds
buckwheat groats (toasted)
sunflower seeds
coconut shreds
bran
wheat germ (toasted)
dried fruit
nuts
pumpkin seeds (toasted)
etc.
add salt to taste.
serve with milk
and honey or
fresh fruit or
yogurt.

SALTY MUESLI -
add chopped dried
umboshi
(japanese salted
plum). omit
milk, coconut,
honey, fruit.

RICE CREAM OR
WHEAT CREAM.

Roast whole grains
in frying pan or
oven. grind up.

to cook - add to
boiling salted water,
one part cereal to
three parts water.

BREAKFAST CEREALS

SPROUTS

any raw whole seed or bean can be sprouted.
Brown rice, soybeans, lentils, wheat, sesame, etc.
alfalfa seeds are good sprouted. By sprouting
grains you can get the nutritional content
without the starch. also sprouts are fresh vegetables
for the winter or for back-packing trips because
they store easily as seeds.

Moisten a clean cloth and cover half of one side
with seeds. Fold over the empty side and put
more seeds on one half of it. Fold over again
and put the cloth in a plastic bag with a
little extra water. Put the bag in a dark place.
Some seeds, like alfalfa, are ready in 4 days. Beans
take longer. another way: place seeds in clean jar, cover
mouth of jar with cloth & rubber band. Every day pour in
some water and let it sit, then
pour it out of jar. Seed must
be moist but not drowning.

133

Sprouts are good in salads, omlets, mixed vegetables and
sandwich fillings.

commercial baby foods are not good for baby. They contain ingredients to please the mother; salt, corn syrup, white sugar, none of these benefit any human body as a steady diet.

Make your own baby food from organically grown fruits and vegetables. Just prepare them so they are soft enough to force through a sieve; use little water so that the vitamin content is not totally destroyed. Fill sterilized (boiled) baby food jars (thrift stores sell empty jars very cheap) or even large canning jars, and process them (see canning).

Make baby cereal from roasted whole grains ground fine in a grinder. Prepare as you would oatmeal.

An ideal first food is mashed fresh bananas. It cures infantile diarrhea. So do strained carrots, strained cottage cheese, and rice cream.

Cow's milk is not a good food for human babies. After baby weans himself, give him soy milk (see recipe) or nut or seed milks (grind nuts or sesame or sunflower seeds and add a little water.) Orange juice is too acid a beverage for his new teeth. A better form of vitamin C is rose hips conserve (see recipe).

Enrich baby's food with soy powder, brewer's yeast, wheat germ oil, lecithin, wheat germ, ground alfalfa sprouts, or molasses. Sweeten only with honey.

BABY FOOD

134

Soy bean curd (tofu)

beat to a smooth paste:
  1 cup full fat soy flour
  1 cup cold water

add 2 cups boiling water and cook 5 minutes over medium heat. add juice of 2 lemons. Remove from heat and let cool. When it coagulates, strain through a cheese cloth until all water drips off. Store in brine and change brine if you store it more than 2 days. To serve, heat gently and serve with sautéed vegetables, tamari and rice.

Soy milk

blend 1 cup soy flour & 4 cups water on top of a double boiler. Let stand 2 hours. Cook 20 minutes, cool, strain. Use residue in breads or porridge. Use milk as milk.

Soy butter

boil together 1 table-spoon soy flour & ½ cup water 'til thick. Strain into a bowl and add soy oil to desired thickness.

also see "macro-burgers" page 131

how to cook a soy bean

Roasted Soy Beans

method 1: soak beans overnight in brine. fry in deep fat 'til they float. drain.

method 2: place soaked or unsoaked beans on a cookie sheet in oven at low heat several hours 'til brown

miso
......
japanese fermented
soy bean paste
(use as a base for
soup, as a sandwich
spread with tahini-
sesame butter - as
a flavoring for
grain dishes -like
soy sauce - salty)

boil 'til soft - soy
beans - and beat
to a smooth paste.
add 3 parts koji
(raw rice - a white
rice used for making

rice wine
& rice vinegar) to
each part soy beans,
and 2 tablespoons
or more of salt

to each cup beans
(taste it - it should
be salty like soy
sauce). Keep in
a cool place. The
rice will turn
mushy and
it will be a smooth
paste. It will
slowly ferment.
Traditionally it
is fermented for
18 months, but
use it when it
tastes right to
you. Commercially

made miso is dark
in color - this will be
light in color.

cooked vegetables are often depleted
of nutrients. boiling vegetables
in water & draining them,
cooking them with "a pinch of soda";
soaking & draining them (raw) and
cooking them slowly all destroy
or cut drastically the nutritional
content. Store vegetables away from light
and heat and don't peel them unless
the skin is tough or bitter.

however, quick cooking does soften the vegetable
and make its nutrients more assimilatable.
before cooking, brush the vegetable with oil to
seal in vitamin C. initial heat should be rapid,
then as the moisture that comprises 75 to 90% of
the vegetable escapes, lower heat, add no water, cook
until sufficiently tender. During lowered heat a
cover should keep steam in. The lowered
heat can also be done in a pre-heated oven with
a pre-heated casserole dish or on top of a
double boiler. Don't let
vegetables cool between
high heat &
low.

VITAMINS & VEGETABLES

VEGETABLE   RECIPES

eggplant: place eggplant on a hot ungreased
flat surface over a hot fire. Don't
peel it or anything. Just leave it
whole. when it turns brown on the
outside, soft in the middle and black
on the bottom, remove the skin and
mash the pulp with some garlic, onion
and salt. Serve hot or cold on chapatis.

greens: put a little oil in the bottom of a big pot-
just enough to cover surface. Brown some
finely chopped garlic. add as many greens as
pot will hold and let them wilt by stirring
into oil. When greens are wilted add more
until pot is about half full of wilted
greens. add _no water_ - there is enough
water in greens to prepare. Continue simmering
over a low flame, covered, until tender.
By greens I mean collards, turnip greens,
mustard greens, kale, spinach and other leaves.

SALADS

place in bowl many different vegetables — wild vegetables
like lambsquarters, sheep sorrel, miner's lettuce, mustard
leaves, or watercress — and some vegetables you
might normally cook like zucchini, broccoli, spinach,
cauliflower — and some taste trips like kelp,
onions, raisins, garlic — and maybe some cold cooked
vegetables or pickled vegetables. Then maybe lettuce and
tomatoes and radishes and avocado. and nuts or seeds.
next toss in some herbs. Now pour on some oil
and mix well. the oil should coat each vegetable.

Just before serving add vinegar or lemon juice and
salt. That way the vegetables won't wilt or lose their
vitamins to the dressing left in the bottom of the bowl.

mix equal parts:
    tahini or oil.
apple cider vinegar
    and season with:
        tamari soy sauce
        garlic juice

SALAD   DRESSINGS

mayonnaise
· · · · · · · · · ·

stir in a bowl for five minutes or more:
    2 egg yolks, 2 tablespoons lemon juice
    or vinegar, 2 teaspoons powdered mustard,
    ¼ teaspoon of salt, and 2 teaspoons of honey.

add one tablespoonful at a time, spaced between
several minutes of stirring, so that the whole
will jell:

    2 cups cold-pressed soy oil or safflower
            oil or olive oil.

when thoroughly jelled and all oil is in, add:

    2 tablespoons lemon juice.

and stir again.

140

nut butters

grind one cup raw nuts at a time to a flour.   add about one part cold-pressed soy or safflower oil to five parts nuts. add salt if desired. Cover & store in a cool place. Brazil, cashew, almonds, filberts have enough oil that   they need less or no added oil.   Allow the grinder to cool between grindings. Clean grinder by grinding up some shredded tissues.

pack the outer compartment of the ice cream freezer with coarse salt and ice. Pour one of the mixtures into the inner compartment, put on the lid and crank for 20 minutes or more until ice cream is frozen. Keep replacing ice as it melts.

honey ice cream

beat 2 egg yolks
add ½ cup honey
    2 cups cream
    1 teaspoon vanilla
    1 cup nuts (optional)
beat 2 egg whites 'til stiff. add to above mixture.

fruit ice cream

whip ¾ cup heavy cream
grind 3 cups fresh fruit
add to fruit: 3 tablespoons honey, juice of one lemon, 1 sprig of mint (ground), ½ cup fruit juice, whipped cream (above).

ice cream

how to smoke fish...

a smoke house should be cool enough so that it doesn't cook the meat. This can be accomplished by funneling stove smoke into a wooden box or by building a little smoke house of cardboard with strips. Reinforce a cardboard carton 2 sets of strips of wood along the corners and near the top on opposing sides, one set near the top and one set near the middle: Cut off the bottom of the box and cut out a door 10 inches by 12 inches folding at the hinge. pierce the box to insert rods (2 at the top to keep the flaps up, 3 just above the upper set of strips and 2 just above the lower set of strips. Place a screen over the lower rods to catch fish that fall.

scale, decapitate and disembowel the fish (leave collar bones.) Soak in brine (4 cups salt to 1 gallon water) 1 hour (or less for little fish). Rinse in clear water, hang on wire and let dry ½ hour or until surface shines. Use heavy wire: under the collar bone, around backbone and up on other side of collar bone. Place big fish on the screen prepare a fire on flat ground of green hardwood sticks 1 inch in diameter (oak, hickory, beech, sweet bay, alder, apple, citrus and corn cobs or coconut husks.) hang fish from the 3 rods above the upper strips. Close the top flaps. Place the box over the fire with door facing wind. Cover all openings and pile dirt around sides (make it airtight). Stoke fire every ½ hour. Check at 3 hours and every hour after that. Fish is done when flesh separates from backbone. Remove house. Cool.

how to salt fish

use non-fatty fish. you will need 20 pounds of salt per 100 pounds prepared fish.

1. to prepare: cut off heads, bleed them, remove guts & black membrane in backbone split in half — if fish is over 10 pounds split again from head to tail.

2. to salt: in a clean waterproof vat sprinkle a layer of salt to cover bottom. Cover with a layer of fish, flesh side up, continue layering fish and salt. Top half of vat place fish flesh side down. The top layer is salt. The salt extracts water from the fish. add more salt if the brine formed will hold more. Leave 12-15 days in warm weather 21 days or more in cold weather. The flesh is translucent and firm when done.

3. to dry: Rinse in fresh brine or unpolluted sea water. Press and flatten fish under weights and boards. Hang fish by their tails or place on racks. Leave in shade one day. Then place in full sunlight six warm days with wind more than 3 m.p.h.r.

4. to cook: Soak overnight with at least one change of water. Use in stew or soup — don't fry. 144

pemmican sausage
. . . .
pound jerked meat to
shreds. melt fat over low
flame. Discard lumps. mix
equal parts grease
and jerky. Pack
into
boiled
clean
guts.

meat

jerked meat
. . . .
cut off all excess fat
and cut long thin
strips. Soak in a
32 to 1 brine or
boiled sea water. Dry
in the sun or
over a smoky fire
(protection from
insects from smoke—
don't cook the meat)
on a rack. Turn
twice a day and cover
at night to keep dry.
It should dry hard
in several days
depending on weather.

after you kill game, cut
the jugular vein and hang
it up by the feet. Eat the
liver the first day and
age the rest 4 days covered
well with cheese cloth.
cooked meat can be preserved
by placing in a clean
covered container and covering
it with hot grease. The solid
grease will protect it.

the truth about soup...

soup is the answer to the
difficulties of the primitive
kitchen. a catch-all for leftovers,
a ready meal for late-
comers. Order of ingredients:
1. boiling water (vegetable cooking water
   or meat stock: see recipe)
2. vegetables raw or cooked, even
   leftover salad (vinegar evaporates)
3. Flavoring ingredients: soy sauce
   or salt, garlic (chopped), herbs,
   brewer's yeast, soy flour, kelp, milk.
4. Starch: grains, beans, noodles,
   potatoes, etc. add in time so
   that they cook their proper time
   and not get all mushy. lumps
   of biscuit dough become dumplings
   in about 30 minutes (boiling hard).
5. See page on "The Wooden Wife from
   Wyoming" (cooking outdoors)

MEAT STOCK

chop bones, disjoint fowl
or rabbit. Sear in hot
fat. Cover with water.
add 1 tablespoon vinegar
per quart water. add salt
& leftover cooked meat if
any is around. cook one
hour, skim surface of
soup until clear. Use
or can while still hot.

Baking Bread

basic recipe for whole wheat yeast bread:

1 package yeast or 1 cake yeast - soak in ¼ cup warm milk with a spoon of honey 'til foamy. Blend: 9 cups whole wheat flour (spring wheat preferably. It's really fantastic if you buy wholewheat berries - $7.00 per 100 pounds - and they don't spoil like flour, either - and grind it yourself the day you bake), 1 tablespoon salt, ¼ cups oil, 3¾ cups warm water or scalded milk, 6 table-spoons honey. Add yeast. Mix well, then knead 10 minutes. cover the dough and let rise in a warm place (like inside a parked car) 2 hours. add more flour to stiffen, knead 20 minutes. Oil a bowl, place dough in, turn it over, let rise 1 hour. Punch down, divide into 2 loaves (or 20 brioche) place in oiled pans, let rise until double (40 minutes maybe). Bake at 325°F for 40 minutes or until bread leaves the sides of the pans. Cool on racks (out of pans).

homemade yeast culture

pare & cube 3 potatoes (¾ pounds), boil in 1¼ cup water 'til tender. Purée potatoes, add cooking water, ¼ cup honey, 1½ tablespoons salt and enough cold water to make 3¼ cups liquid. When lukewarm add 1 cake dried yeast. Let stand overnight. (Use all but one cupful for baking (store under 85°F).

147

unleavened bread (macrobiotic): mix 3 cups whole grain flour per loaf, with 1½ cups water and 1½ teaspoons salt. bake on an oiled pan 1½ hours in moderate oven.

substitutions (for either yeasted or unyeasted):
for each cup whole wheat flour, you can substitute:

  1 cup   potato flour
  1 cup   buckwheat flour (very heavy)
  2 cups   oat or rye meal
  1 cup   rye flour
  1¼ cups white flour
  1⅙ cups rice flour
  1⅙ cups corn meal (good with buckwheat)
  1 cup   soaked whole grains or cooked cereal (decrease water)

and you can add, for each cup whole wheat flour:

  1 tablespoon soy flour, wheat germ, nutritional yeast and/or dry milk.

other nutritional and flavoring agents:
- bone meal
- rice polishings
- sunflower or sesame seed meal
- dried chopped fruit (flour it first)
- grated citrus peel
- chopped nuts
- soy grits
- ground roasted soy beans
- bran
- sprouts
- carob powder
- grated carrots
- coconut
- molasses
- yogurt

148

ratio for biscuits
. . . .
1 part salt
1 part baking powder
6 parts oil or fat
48 parts flour
sufficient water or milk
to make a soft dough
optionally the additions
listed under "breads"
or ½ part herbs (rosemary
    thyme) or spices -
or 6 parts grated cheese
   or finely chopped onions
   or parsley etc.
. . . .
Sift together dry
ingredients, cut in
oil and gradually
add liquid. Roll out
& cut with a cutter
or a glass or pinch
off lumps for
dumplings or
on top of a pan
of fruit & honey
(cobbler), or roll
out ½ inch thick and
cut squares to fold over
and seal shut over a
cooked meat or fruit filling,
or roll out, spread with honey & spice
& nuts, roll up as a jelly roll & bake,
sliced or unsliced. Bake at 350°F until brown.

quick breads

ratio for batters, etc.
. . . .
muffins: add one beaten
egg for each cup flour
and liquid enough
for a lumpy batter.
fill greased tins
½ full, bake 15
minutes at 425°F

pancakes: same as
muffin batter but
increase oil to
12 parts. Cook on
a very hot greased
griddle. Turn them
when all their bubbles
burst.

noodles & pasta: with
a variety of cake icing
presses you can make
fancy shapes. 1 part salt,
1 part brewer's yeast, 96 parts
flour (can be all soy), 2 egg yolks
per cup flour, water for a soft
dough. Press out or roll out thin,
let dry, & cut out strips. Drop
into boiling soup or dry well & store.

sesame crackers: 1 part
flour, 1 part sesame seeds,
salt to taste, water to make
a soft dough. Press ⅙ inch
thick on a greased pan.
Bake 15 minutes at 400°F.

coffee cake: mix one cup flour, one egg, one cup wheat germ or cornmeal, ½ teaspoon each: salt, baking powder, cinnamon, ½ cup each: honey and oil. moisten with enough water to make a stiff dough. Form balls 1 inch in diameter, roll them in cinnamon, wheat germ, and brown sugar; place on an oiled pan, touching, bake 'til dry *

Shirkand: place yogurt in a muslin bag and hang the bag up overnight so all the water drips out. Force the yogurt through the muslin into a bowl. Add rosewater, powdered cardamom seeds and honey that has been warmed a little. (from India).

apple pizza: prepare a dough of whole wheat flour, rolled oats, salt, water, grated lemon peel, cinnamon a little honey and oil. Oil an iron skillet and press dough over bottom of pan ¼ inch thick. Cover with apple slices. Dissolve together honey, lemon juice, cinnamon, & apple juice (a spoonful) over low flame. Pour over pizza. Optional: top with cheese slices. Bake in moderate oven 'til dry.*

earth day cake...

*"dry" means when a knife is inserted in the dough it comes out clean.

Campfire cake: cut an unsliced loaf of bread into big cubes. Dunk in condensed milk, roll in coconut, spear with a green stick and toast over open fire.

Simple Sesame Halvah: grind fine some sesame seed meal and mix with an equal portion of honey. Stir in nuts (chopped) and bits of dried fruit. Thicken either by adding powdered milk or a little flour and stir over a double boiler 10 minutes. Form into cakes and chill.

Recipe for country pie:
pick some fruit, wild
fruit like huckleberries
or blackberries, or tame
organically grown fruit.
cut it up or cut out pits
or whatever has to be
done to it. Dissolve 2
tablespoons Kuzu (arrowroot
starch) in juice of ½ lemon.
add to fruit. add some
honey if it's too tart. Pour in
pie shell, cover with top crust
and bake in

LOVE THAT COUNTRY PIE

moderate oven 'til crust is
golden brown and fruit is bubbly.
(about 50 minutes at 400°F).

crust:

sift together 2 cups pastry
flour & 1 teaspoon salt. Pour
over ½ cup light oil and
¼ cup milk or water. Mix
and form into 2 balls. Place
one ball on a square foot of
wax paper, roll out 'til it meets
the edges. Peel back top layer
of wax paper, place crust in pan,
remove second sheet, trim edges.

roll out second ball the same
way. Place over filled pie,
peel off top layer of waxed
paper. mash down edges with
a fork to unite 2 crusts.
Punch air holes in top crust.
Or cut strips & latice them
(above). or bake tarts in muffin tins.

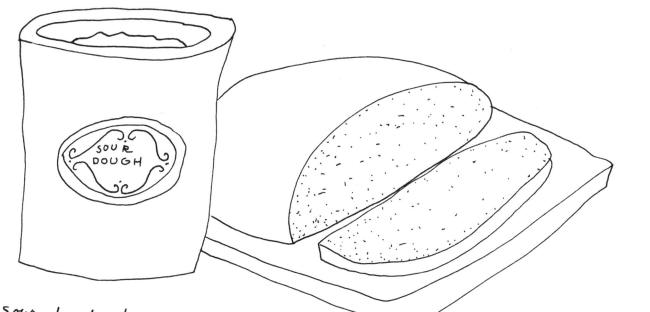

sour dough starter ..... mix: 1 cup flour, 1 cup water, 3 teaspoons yeast, 1 tablespoon honey. Set 5 days in a warm place. Then store under 85°F in a wooden or earthenware pot. It will keep indefinitely in a cold place. If it gets too sour from infrequent use add one cup flour and one cup water (warm).

the night before ..... you intend to bake, combine your starter (one cup) with 2 cups warm water, sift in 2½ cups flour and beat well. Use a glass or earthenware bowl. Cover and leave 12 hours in a warm place (take it to bed with you if you live in a tent). If it stands 36 hours in a warm place it will be more tangy & fermented. Then, before you add any other ingredients, return one cup of batter to the pot as your next starter.

pancakes and waffles ..... to the fermented batter add an egg, a little oil, and sift in a teaspoon each of salt, baking soda, and a little melted honey. Mix well and leave a while to foam up (griddle or waffle iron should be very hot and well greased).

biscuits and doughnuts ..... to fermented batter add 1 cup flour and sift over it ½c. flour, a teaspoon of salt and, optionally: a teaspoon of baking powder, some honey, wheat germ, sesame seeds, sunflower seed meal, spices and raisens, rolled oats (reduce flour if you add grains). For biscuits, dip in oil and place, touching on a pan, let rise 30 minutes and bake 375°F ½ hour. For muffins or cookies, place in muffin tins or cookie sheets. For doughnuts, after rising, drop into hot oil.

bread ..... let starter stand at least 14 to 36 hours. You won't even need salt if it's sour enough. Add enough flour so you can knead it vigorously. Let it rest 10 minutes. Form loaves. Let rise 'til double and bake 20 minutes at 400° in a greased pan. Then lower heat to 325°F and bake until it shrinks from sides of pan.

152

a list of good things to
supplement your diet:

cereal: wheat germ (vitamins
B & E, "complete" protein*) soy grits
(high protein*) sunflower seeds (vitamin E)
sesame seeds (vitamin E) buckwheat
groats (rutin - helps absorb vitamin C)

for soup: brewer's yeast (complete
protein *, B vitamins, minerals), kelp
(all minerals, especially iodine)

vegetables: alfalfa sprouts (vitamins
A, C, B, E, K, and minerals), parsley
watercress, kale, collards, mustard
greens, spinach, turnip greens, comfrey
(large amounts vitamin A, also C).

spices & savouries: paprika (vitamins
A & C, potassium), chiles (A & C), coriander
and cumin seeds (calcium, iron & A),
garlic, apple cider vinegar (both strong
intestinal disinfectants) honey (calms
nerves, energizes), blackstrap molasses
(B vitamin) carob (minerals). (note: molasses
and hot water makes a good beverage).

* a complete protein has all the amino acids.

a list of good things
you can pick yourself:

vegetables: sheep sorrel (a
common weed in gardens, good
in salads, has a sour taste), dandelion
greens (pick within a day of leaves emerging
in spring. Otherwise they are bitter. The
roots can be roasted, ground, and used as
a coffee substitute.) miner's lettuce grows
in wet places, very tender, a little like
spinach heart-shaped leaves have stem through
the center). Watercress grows in streams and
turns bitter after it goes to seed. Otherwise it is
pungent. lamb's quarters cook up like
spinach. It grows in gardens. , Mustard
grows on roadsides everywhere. the early leaves,
the young seed pods, the mature seeds (ground up),
are all edible. Bracken, the most common fern,
appears in early spring and unfolds from a
"fiddlehead" covered with brown fuzz into a
single fern. The fiddleheads are good
cut up in salads and cooked like asparagus.
Purslane is another garden weed that can be
boiled up as a green. More ⟶

nasturtium leaves: have a hot minty taste.
   Easy to recognize by bright orange flowers on
   low green vine and scalloped oval leaves.
   wonderful in salads & sweet sandwiches.
acorns: really tedious to prepare but worth
   the experiment. Crack shells and soak for
   24 hours, changing water every 2 hours (or
   leave in a basket in a stream 24 hours). Shell
   and boil, changing water every hour, until
   bitterness is gone. Use as a bland porridge or
   dry and use as a flour. Very bland.
berries: on blue-berry and huckleberry bushes, just
   place a plastic sheet under bush, and shake the bush.
   raspberry-type berries have to be gathered by hand..
nettles: gather in spring when young and tender.
   They sting, so, you must wear gloves, cut with
   shears. Stem them, boil or steam like spinach.
   This removes the formic acid. The water is a good tea
   or even a hair rinse if you have any left
   after boiling greens.
bark: strip off inner layer of bark of birch poplar
   or lodgepole pine. Chew it raw or in stews.

maple syrup: you will need a brace & bit, a hammer, a spout heavy enough to hold the bucket, and a bucket with a lid. Metal buckets are easier to clean, wooden buckets help prevent fermentation. The latter should be soaked overnight to make the wood tight. Tap after a frosty night in early spring. The sap flows for 5 to 6 weeks. Make a hole 2 inches deep (don't injure tree), insert spout, and hang on bucket. Collect sap in a cauldron and boil it down. It takes about 40 gallons of sap to make a gallon of syrup (about 11 pounds per gallon). Strain syrup through cheese cloth and clarify by adding an egg white and ½ cup milk. These attract the impurities. Boil, skim surface, and pour into sterilized jars. Seal.

156

Seafood:

mussels are edible november through april. Scrape the "beard" off before cooking: boil an inch of water at the bottom of a cauldron. Place mussels in when they burst open they are ready. Serve with butter & garlic sauce.

clams may be dug year round but the stomach (soft dark part inside triangular foot) should be discarded may through october. Rinse in ocean water (fresh water makes them shut tight) and let them rest so they will open their shells a crack. Slide in a knife & cut the abductor muscle. Rinse under cold running water to remove sand. Lift clam from shell with knife. Dip in flour & fry in butter.

small fish with lots of bones when soaked one hour in a solution of vinegar & soda become boneless.

raw fish (sashimi) salt fillets & leave 20 minutes in a collander. Slowly pour water on until flesh is firm. Serve on lettuce with grated radish & ginger.

kelp:

small fronds:
3-10 inches long

midribbed frond:
1-10 feet long
1-3 inches wide

raw in salads: cut thick midrib from long frond and remove membrane. Slice midrib into salad.
dried: (konbu) rinse & dry in sun the small fronds. Dip in boiling water, pressed out flat. Stack them. Put a weight on top to press out excess water. Place cake to dry in oven at lowest heat. When dry, shred with a sharp knife, pack into jars and set jars in oven until warm. Seal jars: the cooling air inside creates a vacuum pack.
To use: crumble to a powder & use for salt. Boil 1 cup konbu in 2 cups water to serve with rice: As soup: 1 tablespoon konbu in 1 cup boiling water & season with soy sauce. In salty crackers: Place a bit in center before baking. 158

cooking outdoors

hints to begin with:
hardwood ash + grease
(animal fat) = soap.
To clean pans, add ashes
& scour. To avoid
black-bottomed-pots:
soap outside of pot
before cooking. The soot
will wipe right off.
soup hole: after hunting
an animal. make a fire
and heat up some stones.
Dig a hole, line with
skin, fur side towards
outside. add water,
salt, bones, wild
vegetables and a
couple of hot clean
stones. Cook 2 hours.
baked in clay: dip
gutted fish or dressed
fowl or vegetable
roots in semi-liquid
clay until well-coated.
place in embers
½ hour. Removal of clay
takes skin feathers
& scales.
fish platter peg
fish to slab of
green hardwood
or a flat rock
and expose
to embers.

159

barbecue: place
green sticks across
big rocks over
embers (at least
4 inches above).
Place meat on grill.
"the wooden wife
from wyoming."
fill a wooden box
with wet alfalfa.
Pack it down tight.
Scoop out a hole and
place your soup pot
inside. Let it dry.
To use it, remove
soup pot and bring
to a boil some water,
chunks of meat, salt,
vegetables. Place
inside box and close
lid. It will continue
to boil all day
while you're
out.

breads
dutch oven is
a big covered
pot with a
rack inside.
Place over fire
with bread pans
on rack.
reflector oven is
a 10 gallon can
cut open facing
fire. (Rack inside)

ground oven is
a hole line with
rocks. Build a fire
in hole. Remove
fire and

place dutch oven
inside hole.
Cover with more
rocks, then dirt.
doughboys. peel
bark off green sticks
leave little branches
to help dough adhere.
roll dough into ropes
and wind around
sticks. Toast over
embers 'til brown.

boiled breads

boston brown bread
soften 1 cake yeast in
2 tablespoons warm sweet
cider. sift together:
1 cup rye flour
1 cup cornmeal
1 cup whole wheat flour
1 teaspoon salt
2 tablespoons nutritional
  yeast or wheat germ
add 2/3 cup molasses
and 1 pint yogurt or
sour milk or buttermilk
and yeast and 1 cup
raisins. Beat well.
Place in an oiled 2
quart container (wide
mouthed). let rise
20 minutes. Steam*
3 hours.

plum pudding
mix: 1 cup each:
whole wheat flour
raisins
chopped almonds
currants
chopped apples
chopped dried figs
chopped dried prunes
chopped dates
wheat germ
honey
and:
2 eggs
2/3 cup milk
3 cups shortening or
  tahini or butter
1 teaspoon each:
allspice, cloves,
coriander, cinnamon
grated orange or lemon peel.
Pack loosely into wide
mouth jars within 1 inch
of top. screw top on tight.
Boil jars 3 hours.

steamed bread
elevate basket
above boiling
water in pot.
Place dough in
basket. * container
of brown bread
can sit in basket.
Pot must have
tight lid.

pan bread
place dough in
greased frying
pan over low heat.
turn every half-
hour.

chapati & tortillas
make a hot flat
surface over the
fire (like a skillet).
Pat out thin rounds
of soft dough
and toast on
surface. Turn
occasionally.

the best kind of cooking pot is a big heavy cast iron skillet with high sides. Heat up oil; have draining plate ready.

Puri: make a soft dough and roll out thin circles. as they cook they puff out into spheres. When drained, poke a hole in the side a fill with sauce.

doughnuts: to every 2 cups flour add one egg, ½ cup honey, ¼ cup oil, 1 teaspoon salt, 1 teaspoon baking powder (optional), 1 teaspoon grated lemon rind, 1 teaspoon cinnamon, & water to form a soft dough. Cut out shapes & fry in fat hot enough to brown a cube of bread in one minute. (see also "sourdough")

Tempura: unusual additions: squash flowers, lotus root, baby green ears of corn, mushrooms, eggs. usual additions: cut up vegetables. water-cress and other wild vegetables.

dip in tempura batter, fry and drain.

batter: whole wheat flour salt and water. add an egg if you know a friendly chicken. Chill if possible batter & vegetables first.

monte christo sandwich: one slice of meat or fowl & some jelly between 2 slices of bread. Dip in beaten egg and deep fry, drain, serve hot.

161

a steam pot has water boiling in the bottom and an elevated container for the food (which is cooked by the heat of the steam rather than by the cooking water). Remember to add water occasionally...

Steamed bread: place bread dough in a collander over boiling water.

steamed vegetables: the vegetables retain more of their vitamins when steamed in a steamer above the water.

steamed mussels: when they are ready they open up a little. serve with butter and garlic sauce.

tamales: mix together cornmeal, water and salt to a thick paste. Spread on dried corn husks and place a little cooked meat or chile beans in the middle. roll up and tie with string and steam ½ hour.

steamed fish: invert a cup in the boiling water and place a plate on top (above the water). Place fish on plate. The fish cooks very quickly and the juices are not lost. Season with tamari soy sauce & ginger.

162

chinese cooking.
. . . .

cleaning brush for wok

wok
stir-fry pan

siou hok
ladle

wok chan
spatula

jing loong
bamboo
steaming
baskets

ting
cauldron

. . . .

imagine yourself high in the green mountains of
china where you have a little hut and a lush
vegetable garden. Your life is vigorous; you waste
nothing. Your kitchen tools are few and simple,
though each serves many purposes. Whatever you
would buy in the far-away village is dehydrated
(dried meat, fish, mushrooms). The wok cooks using
the least fuel most efficiently, because the time spent
cooking is minimal, while the preparations for cooking
take time. This also preserves the nutrients in the
food.   The steaming baskets hold
several separate   foods (rice, vegetables) over the
same heat. Each   meal is subtle art.

choy doh   jahm bahn
chopping   hardwood
knife   chopping block

PEACE

felafel are the arabic taco.
pita is a flat yeast bread - hollow in the middle. In it you put deep-fried balls of garbanzo bean purée, over that a salad of tomato, onion and cucumber or else eggplant cooked according to the recipe in this book, and over that a sauce of garbanzo purée and garlic.

pita

dissolve one teaspoon yeast in ¼ cup warm water with one teaspoon sugar. When foamy add a beaten egg, and 2 cups flour sifted with a pinch of salt, and 3 tablespoons oil and ⅓ cup warm water. Cover and let rise 'til it doubles. Form 12 flat cakes and place on a greased & floured pan. Let rise until double again, pat them flat, brush with oil and bake 20 minutes at 375° until light brown and puffy.

Nahit Sauce

mix together:

1 one cup garbanzo purée
½ cup cooking liquid from beans
4 tablespoons tahini
¼ teaspoon raw garlic juice.

an israeli - arabic recipe...

felafel:

Combine the following and roll into balls one inch in diameter:
4 cups puréed cooked garbanzo beans
1 teaspoon salt
½ teaspoon white pepper
one mashed pickled red pepper
½ teaspoon basil & thyme & marjoram -
    mixed
½ cup fine crumbs
4 eggs
4 tablespoons tahini (ground sesame)
Roll balls in one cup dry crumbs and deep fry.

164

good tasting herbal teas with nutritional value

red clover
shave grass
desert grass
alfalfa
camomile
peppermint
watercress
stawberry leaf
yerba buena
sarsaparilla
rose hip
carrot leaf
nettle leaf
comfrey leaf
yarrow
sassafras

milk dulls aroma & flavor
of tea. Sweeten with honey.
Warm teapot by scalding before
adding herb & boiling water.

cinnamon
apple dishes,
sweet pickles,
sweet fruity
dishes, chocolate,
rice pudding.

rosemary,
for poultry,
lamb, pork,
biscuits, dump-
lings & stuffings.

cumin
mexican food,
especially beans,
indian foods,
salad dressing

dill seeds
for pickles,
sauerkraut,
apple pie

savory
beans & peas,
salads and
vegetable
dishes

nutmeg
use fresh
ground in
custards, milk
& cheese dishes
& eggs.

marjoram
lamb & mutton
dishes, soups,
casseroles,
cooked greens,
yellows & beans.

paprika
hungarian
paprika is best.
In creamed meat,
mushrooms &
goulash, salads

dill weed
eggs, sour
cream & cheese
fish, salads,
veal & meat
pies.

mint
in yogurt,
vegetable
dishes, cold
soups, drinks,
ice cream.

cloves
sweet, spicy
pickles, cakes,
meat dishes,
whole in hot
wine & cider.

thyme
cream sauces,
meat & fish
dishes (use spar-
ingly - team it
with bay leaf).

fennel
soup, fish
& salad (herb).
seeds as a tea,
bulb as raw
or cooked vegetable,
easy to grow.

bay leaves
boil one leaf
in stew, soup,
sauces, remove
before serving.

curry,
grind together:
turmeric, car-
damom, cor-
iander, all-
spice, mustard

allspice
meat dishes,
catsup, spice
cakes, pickled
fruits, curry

basil
salads, tomato
dishes & sauces.
Beautiful grow-
ing in a pot.

garlic
salads, meats,
vegetables, cheeses,
eggs, garlic bread,
sauces & soups.

caraway seeds
rye bread, in
cabbage, beets, &
potatoes, cheeses,
salads, cookies

**juniper
berries**
game,
sauerkraut,
veal & lamb

ginger
like allspice,
also chinese
vegetables, ginger
bread, ice cream

sage
poultry, pork,
veal, cheese,
dumplings and
stuffings

tarragon
flavoring a
vinegar for salads,
also chicken,
eggs, veal, &
prawns

chiles
whole & powdered
in mexican dishes,
coatings for fried
food, creamed
vegetables

mace
cherries,
cakes, cookies,
chocolate,
spiced fruit,
spiced meats.

cardamom
curry, pastries,
in coffee,
flavor
yogurt

oregano
in italian,
mexican &
spanish dishes.
also fish & vegetables

anise
imparts a
licorice flavor
to cookies, bread,
brandy & meats.

coriander
spicy. for
meats, curry,
bland cheese,
artichokes

sorrel
sour leaves
go well in
soup, salad,
fish, & greens.

fresh herbs

pick herbs in summer just when
they begin flowering. Wash gently in a
collander to remove dust and place
on a screen to dry in the sun, or
hang in bunches in hot shade or in
a bag (right→).

If you use fresh herbs in a preparation,
use three times as much fresh herb
as you would dried herbs.

Fresh ginger root can be stored
in a ceramic pot with wet sand
(water every few days).

herbal preparations

gather herbs in the morning before the dew
evaporates off them. to dry them, place upside
down in a paper bag and hang it in a warm
dry place for a few days. Store leaves in jars.
. . . .
infusion (tea of leaves or flowers): pour one pint
    boiling water over 1 ounce herb. Let it sit
    20 minutes, strain. (always cover to steep)
decoction (tea of root, bark, or seeds): boil 30 minutes
    one ounce herb in 1½ pints water, strain.
    You should get 1 pint decoction
powdered or fine cut herbs: prepare infusion using
    one heaping teaspoon per cup boiling water.
. . . .
tincture: let stand, covered, 2 weeks: 4 oz. water,
    12 oz. spirits (not rubbing alcohol) 1 oz. powdered herb.
    Shake well every night. Strain, discard sediment
    and bottle for use (after two weeks it is ready).
poultice: crush fresh leaves or bulbs or mix powdered
    herb with water to form a paste. apply on gauze
distillates: incense oils, rose water, etc. see page
    on distillation.

168

antiseptic : tincture of myrrh

mix and let stand one week:
one quart grain alcohol
½ ounce powdered capsicum (red pepper)
2 ounces powdered myrrh.

myrrh is a very powerful disinfectant. use a few drops of the tincture in a glass of water as a cure for throat infections or a mouthwash. apply tincture directly to sores and wounds to cure or prevent infections.

concentrated antiseptic for backpacking

sold in all drug stores under the name "Roccal", benzalkonium chloride can be diluted 1000 to 1 with water to use as an antibacterial agent.

Other disinfectants:
charcoal powdered and applied to sore.
ear-wax is a natural antibiotic
1 part powdered myrrh to 4 parts vaseline
1 part powdered myrrh and 3 parts charcoal.

Orange-Flower Water

use 3 parts water to one part orange blossoms and distill off two-thirds the amount of water you started with.

Rose-Water

use five parts water to one part washed rose petals. distill off one half the amount of water you started with.

check the cup often to empty it & replace ice cube. Equal parts glycerine & rosewater is a handcream.

distillation on the stove →

pot must be inert - crockery, glass, stainless steel, <u>not</u> iron or aluminum!

← bowl or upside-down dome lid filled with ice so that steam condences on the bottom

← cup placed so that whatever is condensing runs into it

brick to elevate cup from fire

water in pot with herb to be distilled.

a cube of ice to be replaced in cup every so often keeps cup cold.

170

if your stomach doesn't feel good the best cure is to fast. However if your discomfort follows a meal have a cup of tea. Peppermint tea dispels gas; fennel, fenugreek seed, golden seal, ginseng, slippery elm, and rose petal (remove white tips) sooth a cranky stomach. For nausea, down some clove tea or 20 drops of essence of peppermint in a cup of hot water. If you think it's food poisoning, drink apple cider vinegar in water (one teaspoon in a cup of water once ever hour). If it's chemical poisoning, take a piece of burned toast (charcoal absorbs toxins), and orange pekoe tea (tannic acid to counteract alkalines) and milk of magnesia (to counteract acid). If it's sea sickness you've got, take some vitamin B-6 or drink 1 cup water with 1 teaspoon essence of peppermint or suck on a lemon. To cure diarrhea, drink blackberry juice, or boil one tablespoon of kuzu arrowroot starch 'til translucent in one cup water, flavor it with soy sauce and down it; or chew up some garlic. Garlic also cures constipation strangely enough, as does licorice root tea, dried fruits, or yogurt. If you have worms, raw garlic also cures that, but you can also use raw brown rice, pumpkin seeds, watermelon seeds, or papaya seeds with honey. Raw unripe (green) papaya will also dispel worms and it contains an enzyme that helps you digest protein if you take it before a meal.

herbal medicine for the digestive tract

171

toothache place hot water bottle on feet. apply to tooth clove oil or salt or fig tree sap or a whole clove.

sore inflammed mouth golden seal root tea (hold in mouth before swallowing.)

chapped lips or hands apply equal parts glycerine and lemon juice. Castor oil overnight smooths hands.

speck in eye: place a flax seed in eye to absorb particle.

tired sore eyes wash eyes with golden seal root tea or passion flower tea.

insomnia & nervousness drink one of these teas: peppermint, passion flower, plantain leaf, chamomile, dandelion leaf, snakeroot (rauwolfia). you can also chew snakeroot. To induce sleep, mix 3 teaspoons apple cider vinegar in a cup of honey and take 2 teaspoons of this each hour. My proofreader, anna, recommends valerian tea

muscles: sprained — apply a paste of sea salt and cider vinegar sore — take a hot bath. spasms, cramps, twitching — 2 teaspoons honey each meal general fatigue: splash body with cider vinegar on rising.

impotence sarsaparilla tea and pumpkin seeds both contain male hormones. Ginseng — chew leaves or raw or dried root.

wounds, abrasions, cuts: bandaid with a comfrey leaf or a slice of lemon or a garlic poultice. apply tincture of myhhr where infection might occur. Clove oil is also antiseptic. Turmeric tea or green papaya will speed healing, clot the blood. Minor cuts heal quickly with an application of castor oil. Open a vitamin E capsule and apply to make scar disappear quickly.

burns: keep a potted aloe vera plant in your house. apply a slice of the fresh leaf to stop the pain and heal the burn miraculously. If you don't have one, apply honey, apple cider vinegar, or peppermint oil.

sunburn: apply aloe vera or a solution of vinegar and water. Take the B vitamin PABA (para-amino-benzoic acid). to prevent sunburn in fair skin, apply PABA in lotion form (available at health food stores). Tannic acid sooths sunburn; boil up some tan oak or commercial tea and apply to skin

stings: apply mud & tobacco, garlic juice, lemon juice, baking soda & water, honey or vinegar.

splinter: sterilize needle in alcohol and dig it out.

ringworm, impetigo, athlete's foot: apply apple cider vinegar full strength.

moles, warts, liver spots: apply castor oil and/or garlic poultice.

bruises & sore muscles: soak a cloth in hot water. wrap around a spoonful of dried herb of wormwood. apply: absorbs pain & discoloration.

psoriasis: drink sarsaparilla tea

rash: apply horsetail plant infusion (soothing).

corns: soak in hot water, apply castor oil, cover with a sock, leave on overnight

pimples: rub on fresh garlic juice

a cold is the time to fast. Drink nothing but fruit juice; if you must eat, have only fresh fruit and vegetables. Take vitamin C, either from rose hip conserve (see recipe) or fresh rose hips or a tea of strawberry leaves, pine or spruce needles, and/or rose hips. For immediate relief in nasal passages, inhale steam. In fact, a hot steam bath will do much to knock out a cold. Stay still, don't try to accomplish any-thing; relax. To open a stuffed-up nose, chew honeycomb for 15 minutes a couple times a day, or puncture the gum blisters on a spruce tree and take 1 tablespoon of their liquid 3 times a day. Drink a lot of liquid. Hot "stinging nettle" tea or fenugreek tea will clear out mucus. Yerba buena tea fights infections; tarragon & cardamom tea will reduce a fever. Raw garlic, either held in the cheeks or well-chewed (with an apple) has a strong germicidal effect. Put a little piece in your ear for an earache or in your mouth for laryngitis or tonsilitus.

Headache remedies: inhale fumes of boiling vinegar (apple cider). apply towels to head soaked in 3 cups hot water and 1 tablespoon essence of peppermint.

To open a stuffed nostril: Tilt your head so the closed nostril is above the open one. Breathe normally through the open one a few minutes. the closed one will open.

CURING A COLD

cough syrup: boil a lemon 10 minutes. Extract the juice. to this add 1 oz glycerine and one cup honey. Stir before taking - 1 teaspoon 3 times a day. Slippery elm tea also cures a cough and is bland as milk.

sore throat: gargle hot salt water or gargle and swallow any of the following: one teaspoon apple cider vinegar in a glass of water, fenugreek tea, sassafras tea, ginger tea, apricot leaf tea or fresh pineapple juice.

poison oak is a pretty plant. Its leaves are in clusters of 3. They are shiney, sometimes red, but mostly green. The oily juice of the plant causes a rash on human skin by forming itchy little bubbles under the skin. These must be "dried out" for the itching to stop.

cures for poison oak or poison ivy:

apply: apple cider vinegar
. alcohol
& poultice of:
. ground-up jewel-weed or
. green bean leaves or
. garlic or
. used tea leaves (contain tannic acid)
. adobe dust & water
. baking soda & water
. manzanita berries
. oat flour & water

& decoction of:
. tan oak leaves
. manzanita leaves
. borax & water
. rolled oats (cooking water)
& tincture of lobelia

if you touch or **scratch** the rash you will spread the poison with your hands. (oh toiture). one can become pretty immune to plant toxins by drinking the water that flows past where they grow. or by eating honey made in the same locale. both contain minute amounts of the toxins.

where to buy herbs if they don't grow where you live

USA

harvest health inc.
1944 eastern ave s.e.
grand rapids michigan
. . . . . .

haussman's pharmacy
6th and girard ave
philadelphia pennsylvania
. . . .

herb products co.
11 012 magnolia blvd.
north hollywood, california
. . . .

indiana botanic gardens
p.o. box 5
hammond indiana
. . . . . .

kerbel pharmacy
1473 bedford ave
brooklyn, new york

merit herb co.
p.o. box 225
south chicago
station
chicago, illinois
. . . . .

nature's herb co.
281 ellis st.
san francisco
california
. . . . .

old fashioned herb co.
81 north lake ave.
pasadena california
. . . . .

puregrade health inc.
25 school st.
quincy massachusetts

CANADA

dominion herb distributors
1447 - 51 St. Lawrence Blvd.
montreal canada

tobe's
St. Catherine's
Ontario Canada

request catalogues

176

Shampoos

prepare infusion of comfrey leaves; steep one hour; strain. Dilute some woolite with this tea to normal washing proportions. Dissolve in this: 2 tablespoons of glycerine per quart. if you want to add a beaten egg, wash & rinse with cold water or the egg will coagulate. Comfrey contains alantoin, an anti-bacterial agent.

fels naphtha and cold water also works just fine.

rinse afterwards with diluted vinegar or lemon juice to neutralize the soap. . . . . . .

to stimulate growth

apply after shampoo a strong tea of indian hemp leaves & water. sorry, smoking won't help.

apply castor oil overnight shampoo next day. (castor oil also makes eyelashes grow thick) brush daily & protect from sun.

how to trim split ends without decreasing length of hair

one at a time, take each lock of hair, twist it up tight, stroke toward scalp. The ends will stick out. Trim them and release.

dandruff cures

boil 5 minutes in a covered pot: ½ cup mint leaves, ½ cup cider vinegar, 1 cup water. cool, apply to scalp after shampoo.

boil slowly 2 hours in a covered pot: 1 cup stinging nettle leaves, 1 quart water. Strain, cool, apply to scalp.

conditioners after shampoo

dip brush in nettle rinse (above). Brush 5 minutes.

apply oil of rosemary on brush to wet hair. Untangles, leaves no scent.

beer with a drop of castor oil. rinse out after a few minutes

mayonnaise (yes). rinse out with cold water.

herbal hair care

for women

menstrual cramps: the knee-chest position (above) tips
the uterus into a more comfortable place.
tampon: a sterilized rubber sponge, cut into
the right shape works in emergencies.
douche: fenugreek tea (known for its mucus
dissolving qualities). Vinegar & water
(disinfects & deodorizes)-1 tablespoon per quart.
pregnancy: golden seal (an herb) tea cures morning
sickness. Vitamin E prevents stretch
marks (take capsule orally). Coffee decreases
absorbtion of vitamin C. a pregnant or nursing
woman needs twice as much vitamin C as
other people. By drinking alfalfa-mint tea
instead, you get calcium & many vitamins.
exercises : With the 2 hatha yoga positions above and
squatting when you move your bowels your
abdomen is strengthened for labor.

CHILDBIRTH AT HOME...

the exercises in the la maze books are the best
preparation as they help you to relax. The things
you'll need are: a clean absorbant mat to lie on,
lots of clean rags, a receiving blanket for the baby,
castor oil, antiseptic, and a sterile blade & sterile
heavy thread for cutting the cord. The traditional basin
of hot water is for bathing the mother afterwards.
When the baby comes out he will be blue until he
takes his first breath. If he has trouble doing so,
hold him upside down, clear his mouth, and tap his
back. Put the baby to the breast and/or massage
the breasts to stimulate contractions that
expel the placenta. Don't wash the baby, leave
on the coating. Apply castor oil to breasts to
increase flow of milk if necessary.

Some women prefer squatting to lying back on a bed.

to cut the cord: Do not cut the cord until it
is white and all pulsation ceases. That way all
its blood will have flowed into the baby. It is not
necessary to cut it; left alone the cord will
179 eventually shrivel up and detach itself from

the baby. If you want to cut it, lessen the possibility of infection by cutting it far from the baby (the extra inches of cord will dry up and disappear). Tie two knots around the cord 2 inches apart with heavy thread. Cut between them.

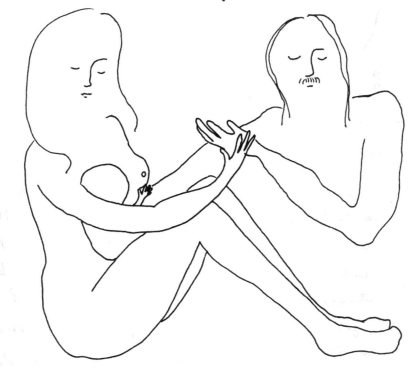

apply castor oil to the navel of the infant if it fails to heal quickly. After the birth the mother may be constipated. Prunes or dried figs will help remedy this. A cup of sarsaparilla tea will quiet the muscles after the birth (contains the hormone progesterone). Navajo women are given watercress as a tonic after a birth. Red raspberry leaf tea has been used in Europe for centuries for the same purpose. It relaxes the vaginal muscles (good also for menstrual cramps). If she can, the mother should eat some of the placenta. 180

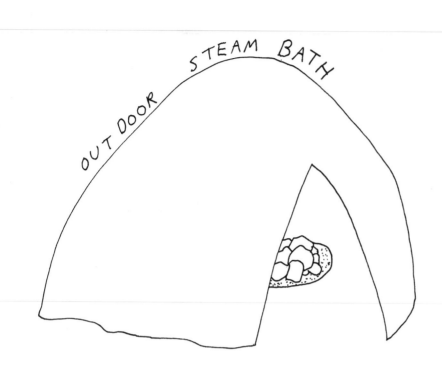

OUTDOOR STEAM BATH

build to preserve heat—
a dome of curved poles
lashed together at the top
and covered with plastic
sheets with a door of
same that opens and closes
easily. Cover floor with
grass and dig a pit in
the center.

Build a bonfire with
rocks (make sure they
are not from a stream
bed as they will explode
when exposed to heat)
stacked up between the
burning sticks and logs.
Fire should burn an
hour or more to heat
rocks thoroughly. Build
fire away from dome
as plastic is flammable.
Remove rocks from
ashes with a pitchfork
and place in bucket. Avoid
getting cinders in bucket
they create smoke in
steam bath.

When all bathers are
inside dome and door
is shut, pour water
on hot rocks. Mint
or yerba buena leaves
can be thrown on rocks
for fragrance.

When bathers have had
enough steam, they
exit dome and run for
a bath of ice cold water
in a stream or lake.

BATHING WHERE WATER IS SCARCE

SUMERIAN BATH

a sumerian bathtub is usually made of stone but you can make one by digging the shape out of sand or loose dirt and lining it with a sheet of plastic. The shape is that of your body and its depth is half the thickness of your body. make it gradually shallower toward the feet. Fill it with water and add a little oil. Now lie in the water fifteen minutes. the back of your body will warm the water and your front will be warmed by the sun. Now turn over. Your circulation gets a rush as the wet side hits the air and the sunwarmed side hits the water. the oil keeps the skin moist. Turn every fifteen minutes.

HERBAL PACK - Boil sheets in an herbal tea (yerba buena is good) and place one on bed over a sheet of plastic. When sheet has cooled enough to lie on - lie down and have someone else wrap you up in the sheet, cover you with blankets and wrap the plastic over you. Sleep in the pack ½ hour and come out & be massaged.

JAPANESE BATH

all you need is one pail of water. Soap your body all over using a little water to make suds. then use a sponge to rinse and scrub your body at the same time. Keep sponging until you are clean and soap-less. Water can be warmed on a sunny day by letting it sit and run through a hose outdoors. An easy water heater can be rigged to a wood-burning stove by making a coil of pipes that covers the surfaces of the stove

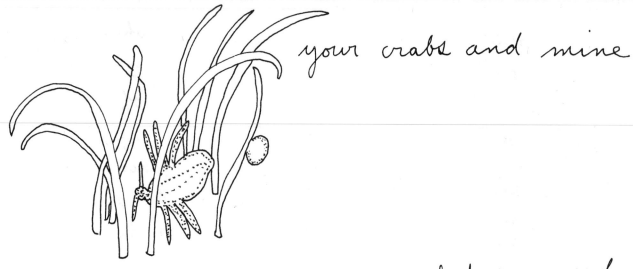

your crabs and mine

above is a crab taking a stroll through a forest of pubic hair. The egg it just laid will hatch in 10 days. the crab is a louse that prefers the pubic hair but will go almost anywhere (eyelashes, underarms) except the scalp. That area is reserved for head lice, a cousin: . They have another cousin, the body louse (or cootie) which can lay thousands of eggs in its short (40 days) sweet life. All are obviously a drag.

If you have tenants in your hair, don't share them. Do them in.

what you need to do in crabs is: a bottle of pyrinate A-200 (kerosene works too, but doesn't kill the eggs so you must repeat in 10 days) a fine-toothed comb and shampoo to wash out the pyrinate. You must take your clothes and wash them in boiling water and put your bedding through the dryer (10¢ at a laundromat). Sprinkle your mattress with flea powder.

tooth brush:
cut a piece of alfalfa
root 6 inches long.

strip off outer skin,
allow it to sun-dry
thoroughly, and
strike one end
with a hammer
to fan out the
fibers.

a whole clove or
gauze soaked in
oil of cloves may
be applied to an
aching tooth as
an anesthetic &
antiseptic.

EGG PLANT
TOOTH
POWDER

cut an eggplant into cubes. wrap each cube
in foil & stick them in hot coals. In about 15
minutes the eggplant will turn black and crumbly.
If it turns white it is too done - discard it.
Mix eggplant powder with equal parts of sea salt.
store in jars. Eggplant cures many gum diseases.
Salt is also very good for the mouth.

In case of a toothache, apply tooth powder to
tooth and try to keep it dry. Even plain salt
will work in toothaches to ease pain.

184

Prolonged exposure to cold: do not bring into warm room at once. Leave patient in a cool place & warm him gradually with blankets & warm drinks. Then put him in a warm bed.

Frost bite: loosen clothes to open circulation. Rub gently with warm hand and cover it up. Never rub with snow

FIRST AID

Burn covering large area of skin: soak gauze or a sheet in one quart boiled water (cool) with 3 tablespoons baking soda. Cover burn with sheet, then cover with a blanket. Never apply iodine

Foreign body in ear: do not attempt to remove it. Take it to a doctor. If it is an insect, pour in a little olive or mineral oil.

185

Snake bite: lie down, keep quiet. Keep bitten limb lower than body. Tie a bandage above bite to cut circulation. Every 20 minutes release and retie. Make X cuts over fang marks (avoid blood vessels) and apply suction with heated cup (sucks as it cools) or by mouth & spit it out. Apply a strong solution of epsom salts in hot water between suctions.

FIRST AID KIT:

bandaids
antiseptic
adhesive tape
gauze bandage
compress
ace bandage
knife
needle

burn ointment
bug repellant
vinegar
clove oil
epsom salts
cup
castor oil

Fractures:

broken bones create a painful swelling and, if the fracture is compound (the bone shatters apart) a wound in the skin. If at all possible, do not move the injured person & wait for a doctor. If you must move him, Bind the limb with a splint first →

Splint:

place board against limb. wind cloth around, tie at each end.

Mouth to Mouth Resuscitation

1. Turn head to side. Clear the mouth of food, mucus, sand, etc.
2. Straighten head & tilt back. Keep jaw jutting out so tongue won't block air.
3. Place mouth over mouth and pinch nostrils.
4. Breathe in so that chest rises.
5. Remove mouth, listen for returning air.
6. If no return, check head & jaw position. if still no air, slap between shoulder blades to clear throat. Repeat #1.
7. Continue breathing in & removing mouth 20 times per minute for an adult or 25 times per minute for a child. 186

Sunstroke   and Heat Exhaustion

Symptoms

red face	pale face
skin hot & dry	skin cool & sweaty
pulse strong	pulse weak
body temerature high	body temperature cool
headache or unconsciousness	short period if any unconsciousness

Treatment

lie down	lie down
elevate head	lower head slightly
cool body with cold compress	keep body warm
do not give stimulants	give salt & water solution and coffee.

massage your eyeballs
by gently placing one
hand over each eye and
rotating it in its socket
(eyes closed.)

EYE EXERCISES

hold up the index finger of each
hand. Look straight forward. Place
fingers as far to each side of you
as you can see. Now alternate
looking at the two fingers.

now alternate looking as far
up and down as you can, still
not moving your head.

Roll your eyes.

187

close your eyes; turn
your head to the right;
open your eyes. Quickly
focus on something
twenty feet away. close
your eyes; turn to the
left; open and focus.

the numbers are to show
the course your eyes take
as they travel from the
inner circle to each outer
circle.

this is a tibetan eye exercise.
focus on the circle in the center.
now travel with your eyes: once around the center
    circle and outward along the dots until you
    reach an outer circle (once around it) and
    follow the dots back to the center (once around
    again) and out to another circle until you do them all. 188

HOW TO AWAIT WATER RESCUE

1. float face down. relax. this is the position you float in naturally.

2. every six seconds, slowly bring one arm & one leg forward.

3. take a breath.

4. relax again. Thus you may survive for a long time as you use little energy.

massage.: a table of waist-height is best. stroke very firmly (but do not pinch) the thickest part of the muscle. Stroke toward the heart when you do the limbs. you may want to lubricate your hands with a vegetable oil, like sesame or soy oil, and scent it with an incense oil like mint. Try not to pick up your hands - have a contin- nuous touch

move your whole body rather than just your hands. when doing the upper back, do the shoulder, neck, biceps, triceps, scalp (rub in circles with fingertips - firmly), side of chest, and as many different things as you can think of to the spine. You can cure a headache by placing your index and third fingers on either side of the spine at the neck and stroking down to the waist with a short fast firm stroke (repeat several times).

the face, hands, and feet require sensitive stroking. The stomach may be stroked across the body. A simple order to work: chest, stomach, tops of legs & arms, hands, feet, face (turn over) back, hips, limbs, feet & hands, scalp.

to die in the forest

cremate on a hot fire
so the smoke
goes straight to heaven
& the ashes
to the four winds
then   a   wake
        the joy of liberation

to cremate
make a pyre of
wood; lay the body
on top, pour on
kerosene and lots
of incense. Burning
bodies don't smell
so good.

191

the book of tao says that every day the Scholar must
know more & more, but the follower of tao
must know less & less. Eventually I must
say 'no' to this unceasing tide of information.
This book is already too
thick. But, if the tide
bends me again, this book
will have a sequel. Besides,
it was fun drawing
all these pictures
   ...A.B.L. OBGFasor

Index

note about the index:

many materials, especially
recycled ones, like cans and
glass containers, are listed
so that you can see their
varied uses throughout the
book.

appendix A
useful addresses

pack frames, hiking boots,
sleeping bags, tents, and
materials & instructions
to make your own:

    sierra designs, inc.
    4th and addison streets
    berkeley california
    (request free catalogue)

leather & leather-working
tools & supplies:
    leather, etcetera
    1609 San Pablo ave.
    berkeley california

non-electric flour
grinders & ice cream
freezers:
    Smithfield implements
    Smithfield, Utah

polyurethane paint:
    ideal paint company
    2200 lombard street
    San francisco california

bulk whole grains, brewer's
yeast, wheat germ, & other
natural* foods:
    *untainted, nutritious

Sonoma natural foods
4411 gravenstein highway north
sebastopol, california
    (also has herbs)

put together instrument kits:
dulcimers, thumbpianos, irish
harps, sitars .... (too much!)
    V. E. Hughs
    8665 W. 13th ave.
    denver colorado 80215

herbal oils, shampoos, lotions
glycerine (neutral) soaps:
    The Body Shop
    1940 Shattuck ave
    berkeley, california

basic H biodegradable
soap (essential if you
care about your pollution.
It also happens to clean
everything very well).
distributor:
    848 california street
    San francisco, california

chain saw:

    homelite carryable
    equipment
    727 airport blvd.
    South san francisco
    california

fire bricks for kiln:

interpace corporation
2230 foothill blvd.
hayward california 94541
(ask for JM 20, 23, or 26 insulating)

wok (stir-fry pan) &
utensils (no cast iron to
be had anywhere, though):

    Ti - Sun Company
    1123 grant avenue
    San francisco, California.

potash, lead carbonate,
lye, chloride of lime,
potassium dichromate,
alum, & other chemicals

    mc kesson chemical co.
    241 quint street
    San francisco california

rotar-tiller:

    home tractor &
    equipment company
    110 howard street
    petaluma, california

foam rubber mattress:
california surplus sales
1107 mission street
san francisco, california

earthworms:

    brazos worm farms
    route 9
    waco, texas 76705

plastic sheets & plexiglass:
transparent products corp.
689 harrison
San francisco, California

paolo soleri:

    cosanti foundation
    6433 East Double tree Ranch Rd
    Scottsdale, arizona

for ceramics & glazes:
leslie ceramics
1212 san pablo
berkeley california

whole earth catalogue
(tools, books, materials
 for every trip) (amazing)
published by Portola Institute
558 Santa Cruz
menlo Park, calif. 94025
. . . .

U.S. department of
agriculture has
pamphlets on all
phases of farm work
(request catalogue)
. . . .

rodale books publish
a variety of
natural health,
nutrition,
organic farming
books - even one
on composting.
rodale publishing,
emaus, pennsylvania
. . . .

nature books
(request catalogue)
naturegraph
press,
healdsburg
california
. . . .

mildred hatch free loan library
8 pine street, johnsbury vermont
(request catalogue)   05819
"loan library on nutrition and some other
essentials of health & creative living...
borrowed books may be kept 2 weeks
for the cost of outgoing postage. Return used
books if you want to buy (no obligation)."

camping books.
skills in taming the wilds
how to stay alive in the woods
home in your pack
we like it wild
how to build your home
     in the woods
on your own in the
          wilderness

wilderness cookery
free for the eating
how to go live in the woods
     on $10 a week
mister rifleman
          all by bradford angier
          published by stackpole books
     . . . .
the indian teepee
          by reginald laubin
     . . . .
the indian how book (1927)
          by arthur C. Parker
          george H. Doran Co.
     . . . .
cache lake country (1947)
          by John J. Rowlands
          W. W. Norton & Co.
     . . . .

at home in the
wilderness
by Sun Bear
Western Printing &
Publishing Co. 1968
     . . . .
going light with
backpack or burro
     Sierra Club 1951
     . . . . . .
light weight camping
equipment & how
to make it (1959)
by gerry cunningham
& margaret hansson
order: gerry P.O. Box 5544
     denver colorado.
     . . . . . .
the complete walker
colin fletcher
     alfred a. Knopf 1969
     . . . .
Camping & Woodcraft
by Horace Kephart
1917 - reprinted 1967
     MacMillan & Co.
     . . . .
be an expert with
map & compass
by bjorn Kjellstrom
american Orienting
Service 1955

books on crafts
. . . .

step by step weaving
    by nell znamierowski
        golden press 1967
. . . .

dictionary of embroidery
    (25¢) women's day magazine
        p.o. box 1000   dept. wd1
            greenwich connecticut
. . . .

rags, rugs, & wool pictures
        by ann wiseman
        scribner's sons 1968
. . . .

"batik"   & "stitchery"
both by nik krevitsky
reinhold books 1966
. . . .

macramé
    by virginia isham harvey
        reinhold books 1967
. . . .

course in making mosaic
by joseph l. young
reinhold books 1957

a potters book
    by bernard leach
faber & faber ltd.
london   1940
. . . .

books on
nutrition, health,
herbal medicine,
cooking, wild
foods, & self-
improvement
. . . .

back to eden
    by jethro kloss
longview publishing
house   1939
. . . .

vermont folk
medicine   by
d.c. jarvis, m.d.
faucett crest books
        1958
. . . .

nature's medicines
by richard lucas
award books 1966

vital foods for total health
by bernard jenson

. . . .

the natural foods cookbook
by beatrice trum hunter
pyramid books 1967

. . . .

the herbalist
by joseph e. meyer
published by
clarence meyer 1960

. . . .

the new child birth (lamaze)
by erna wright
hart publishing co. 1966

. . . .

natural health & pregnancy
by j. i. rodale
pyramid books 1968

. . . .

child birth
by john seldon miller m.d.
atheneum 1966

. . . .

get well naturally
by linda clark
arc books 1969

. . . .

the easy way to chinese cooking
beverly lee   double day 1963

by adelle davis:

let's get well
let's cook it right
let's eat right
        to keep fit
let's have healthy
        children

published by
harcourt brace
        & world

. . . .

by euell gibbons:

stalking the
        wild asparagus
stalking the
        blue-eyed scallop
stalking the
healthful herbs

published by
david mckay

. . . .

el molino mills
best recipes
cookbook
(consumer services
of el molino mills)

Sense relaxation
  (below your mind)
bernard gunther
collier books 1968
(a beautiful guide for
group experience)
. . . .

summerhill
  by a. s. neill
  hart publishing co.
  1960
(about a famous
"free school" in
england by its
founder & leader)

. . . .

herbal handbook for
farm & stable
by julliette de bairacli ley
faber & faber ltd.
london   1963

. . . .

ball blue book of
home canning (35¢)
Ball Bros. Muncie, Indiana

some common
mushrooms &
how to know them
by Vera K. Charles
(35¢) dept. of
agriculture
circular 143
superintendent
of Documents
Washington, D.C.
. . . .

grow your own
(organic
  gardening book)
jeanie darlington
bookworks 1970
. . . .

teaching montessori
in the home
by elizabeth hainstock
random house 1968
(learning games for
children 2-5. Teach
reading at home! ....)
. . . .

the organic morning
glory message (15¢)
(monthly magazine)
71 delmar street
san francisco california
  94117

magical books

mio, my son
by astrid lindgren
charlotte's web
by e. b. white
pippi long-stocking
by astrid lindgren
stuart little
by e. b. white
wind in the willows
by kenneth grahame
winnie the pooh
by a. a. milne
the borrowers
by mary norton
the hobbit
by j.r. tolkien
the cat in the hat
(and about 50 other
great books)
by dr. suess
the pot of gold
by james stephens
fairy tales
by hans christian
anderson
the oz books
by l. frank baum

the little prince
by antoine de
st. exupery
fables & fairy tales
by leo tolstoy
the lord of the rings
by j.r.r. tolkien

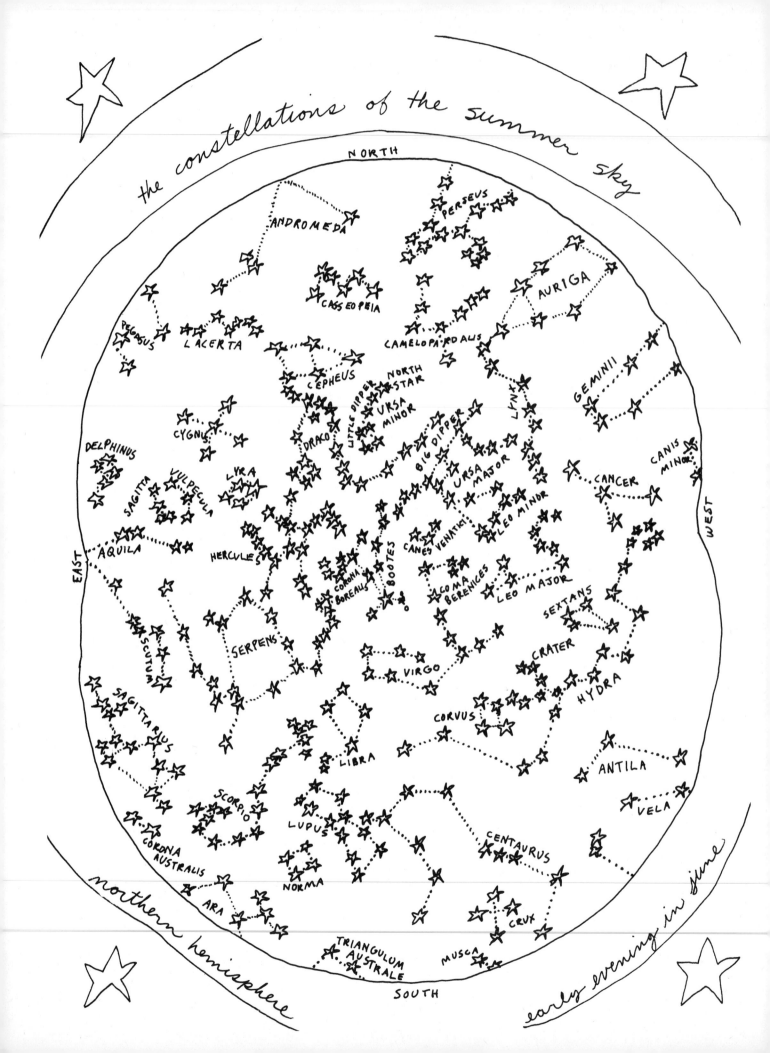

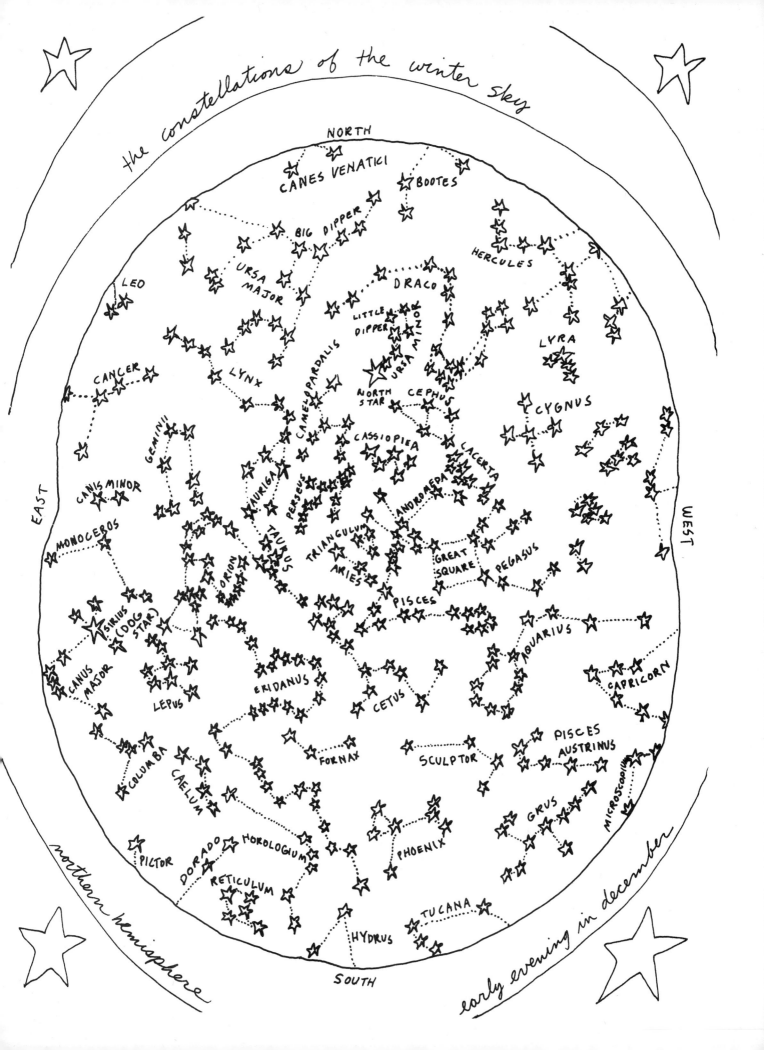

the MOON rises when the sun goes down
when it is full.
the MOON rises with the sun
when it is new.
the MOON as she waxes rises later
and later in the day.
the MOON as she wanes rises later
and later after sundown.
I see the moon and the moon sees me.
God bless the moon and God bless me.